Monsters &

Nick Yarris

ISBN: 1722170697
ISBN-13: 9781722170691

DEDICATION

I dedicate this work to Harriet "Jayne" Yarris. It was you who inspired me to find whatever that is good and decent about myself. You stuck by me 'Sport' and that meant the world of difference to me while I was going through my bleakest of times. I will never let go of my vow to you to always be a nice man. The rest I see now, is just my being part of life with dignity. It is down to me to put perspective on who I am in that context.

CONTENTS

ACKNOWLEDGMENTS

I would like to acknowledge my younger self for having the poise and dignity within to find the courage to rise above my situation.
I go around the world praising others who develop well regardless of what they had to face in life. I should then acknowledge my own advancements in life just as unabashedly as I give praise in this way.

So to you young Nick Yarris, I thank you for allowing me the chance to use the time spent while in prison to now have a purpose in sharing my life with so many humans today.

1. 'NO WAY ARE WE LETTING *THESE* MEN OUT OF THEIR CELLS'!

Pittsburgh Penitentiary January 1995. It is early afternoon.

This story begins within an enclosed setting located inside of the interior of a brand new specially designed "PSYCHIATRIC DEATH ROW UNIT" perched high atop the main prison buildings within the Penitentiary compound itself. It was a unit made initially for punishment and administrative segregation for prisoners who were violent or in need or protection. The building was odd...3 stories high, yet split on 5 levels (with the upper most part surrounded in heavy wire), it was intimidating.

The only way in or out of the top level was a slow elevator connecting the unit to the ground floor. Once inside of this rickety box that was about 5 feet squared, you felt trapped within it. It was all part of a unit that was a hell-hole all of its own design like that.

Here is the prelude to this all being the setting for this story...

In 1993 Pennsylvania opened Greene County Super-Max Prison. It was built in the furthest Western part of the state, located some 60 miles Southwest of Pittsburgh, so this was a place to isolate physically.

Within 2 years of opening its main housing units to general population prisoners, the new "Super-Max" unit located within this prison would be one of two central Death Row units the state used going forward.

At the time of this event, 225 men were under sentence of death in Pennsylvania. The majority of the men expected to go to Greene County prison were those men who came from Huntingdon Prison, located in Central Pennsylvania. This ancient relic in the system had just been ordered by the Federal courts to transfer the 154 of the men housed there on Death Row which it held, all be gone by January 1995.

At some point the Pa. Department of Corrections had to decide which inmates were to be housed at which prison for both security and function. The courts mandated that the antiquated system of 23 hours a day solitary confinement was to be halted. That men sentenced to die deserved to be out more.

The new unit in Greene County had day-rooms and recreational areas set up to allow controlled times of up to 8 hours per day for Death Row men to be let out of their cells.

While the usual concerns of separating inmates who had testified against fellow Death Row prisoners mandated that a lot of the decision to transfer men was security related. That was a small group. Then there came a point where the administration balked at the "Monsters and Madmen" they held being allowed out of their cells.

The idea of serial killers with convictions for killing numerous victims being allowed out of their cells to interact with the mentally weak was scary. What about the cannibals who became even more aggressive after years of torment from fellow inmates? Then what to do with men who had assaulted staff, raped other inmates in the past, or were on heavy medications to curb their psychosis?

No, there had to be some place truly isolated for the worst case men to be held while Pennsylvania tried to comply with the courts. No way could Pennsylvania risk serious incidents in a new prison meant to be a very new statement about Pennsylvania and its modern penology. An idea was then put forth to segregate the "worst of the worst" in the old Pittsburgh Penitentiary.

There, in a sealed unit that was inaccessible to the main prison, they would begin the first ever "Psychiatric Death Row" unit. There were 46 cells and two "Death Watch cells" set up in Pittsburgh for what would soon be the setting for this experiment. The State was claiming that the 48 men whom they picked out could be held back from the courts orders because they were all too deranged to act accordingly.

Now, for whatever reason there is, with 48 new Death Row men being transferred to Pittsburgh prison, there had to be a selection of the staff who would be running the unit. This factor, more than any other one thing, led to so much madness afterwards. It was the men working there who would be in charge of 48 mentally ill, violently deranged Death Row prisoners they were told going in. These guards who were the least equipped mentally to handle this unit, is what then led to a complete breakdown of control.

The average prison guard working on this unit had numerous infractions or complaints filed on them for abuse by prisoners. They were used in this disciplinary housing setting for their ability to conduct brutal reprisals for inmates who acted out. Thugs with clubs who had no compunction or hesitation to inflict pain, these men were not trained to deal with psychosis.

These men were not given extensive training in the understanding of mental illness. They were in no way equipped to handle men meant to be in a psychiatric hospital, and they treated all 48 men as if they were in need of punishment.

When one combines the worst of the worst prisoners condemned to die, along with with deeply disturbed minds of prison guards who have shown a propensity for violence, the outcome would of course be chaos.

In 1995 no one conducted psyche tests on the staff of a new unit inside of this prison to see how they would react to being around a man who would laugh in their faces about how he had butchered a disabled child. No one took the time to evaluate the men who would have to be around a man who had tortured women and was racially driven by this. The administration used guards from the "hole" (or punishment settings) to then treat mentally disturbed men. No one considered the "Princeton Experiment" to take place, because this had not been tried before.

Now, how did I end up being able to tell you all of this story? Let's just say that I was deemed one of the most likely Death Row prisoners housed in Pennsylvania in 1995 to be sent to a nuthouse like this. I fit all of the criteria. Violence on my record, convicted of a psychological based murder, having escaped Death Row briefly in 1985, it was a no-brain decision that I was being sent there.

The day that all 48 men were placed on a prison security bus to be transferred out of Huntingdon prison (where I had just spent the previous 12 years lock up inside of) was eerie for me personally.

On the way *into* Huntingdon in 1983, I was the only Death Row man on the bus full of prisoners. There were only 27 men in the whole State of Pennsylvania sentenced to die at the time. As I left that day in 1995, I was a middle aged man witnessing my own growth from when I first landed, to when they finally shut that place down. I felt sad that I would lose all of my comforts and ability to have a set routine. I had no clue what was waiting on me next while I had 3 men on the bus who had tried previously to murder me. To sit with your arms and legs restrained for hours on a bus with men known for their ability to get out of their restraints to kill or maim was a marathon exercise of being prepared for an attack.

I was also wearing 50.000 volts of electrical charge strapped to my kidneys on a thick leather belt as I was a former escapee, so I also had to deal with what would happen if anything kicked off and I was electrocuted. It would be a horror if I got zapped by the guard holding the remote controlled activator of my restraint due to a fight. I sat quietly and kept myself alert to things, but each man seemed so muted and scared of what was waiting on us all at the end of this ride, that no one spoke the whole way.

When the guards surrounded the bus once it had stopped fully inside the walls of Pittsburgh Penitentiary, there was dead silence for a long period.

There must have been 25 prison guards or more, all of whom were in heavy gear. They started taking one man between two guards and marching them off of the bus and into the new unit which they would be now housed inside of.

I was glad that unlike my very first bus ride into Death Row, that I did not get a beating and thrown into a cell. This time it was all part of numerous men being taken inside and I was no bother to anyone at first. Within 40 minutes of the bus pulling up to the gates of Pittsburgh, all 48 men had every nook and cranny of their body searched and put into a cell.

Now I want to go back into that frame of mind which I had to have back then to survive. I am going to take you with me into this ordeal in that way and stick to how my perspective was driven through it all.

Before now I deliberately did not want to share all of this story for the personal pain which it holds for me even now. Hard to believe that after I have told so much of my life previously, that this one segment of time stole so much of my efforts to tell of my development. I had tried previously to just write it all off as a waste of time. I guess that just goes to show me now once more that everything happens for a reason, and that in time what we hold onto fiercely will change later as well.

So here goes, from day one of my entry into being labeled one of the "Monsters and Madmen" who were subjected to this pitiful experiment...

I am standing in a prison cell that is made of cinder blocks which are painted light blue. I have a gray painted sliding metal door facing me that has a flap cut into it called a "Pie-Hole" that is about 24 inches long, and about 6 inches high. It's waist high on the door. There is an additional cut in the door about 4 inches wide, by 22 inches high (with mesh screen covering these openings). This is to allow staff to see into and speak to prisoners without your "Pie-Hole" being open. These cuts are designed so your door to the cell never cuts off sound or air flow. It is also through these upright cuts on the doors that you can see outside of your cell to the surrounding cell area nearby.

I am wearing only an orange jumpsuit, thin white T-shirt, white boxers shorts and blue canvas prison issued shoes with white rubber soles and brown socks. The 2 upright cuts in each cell door that have heavy metal wire crisscrossed into diamond patterns. The outside area is in a weird pattern that your eyes have to adjust to then make sense of what you are seeing. At least one of your eyes has to look past metal wire to focus and it's annoying to have to try this while wearing corrective eye glasses I find.

I look to my right on the wall inside of my cell and I see that there is a metal speaker cover for the intercom/speaker/microphone bolted there.

This is where the guard inside of a glass control booth located out in the hallway will talk to me. I can see the control booth windows and a single guard standing inside of it. I will speak to that officer while I am locked inside of my 6 foot wide by 8 foot long cell.

I look to my right inside of my cell over to the metal toilet that has a sink with taps fitted atop of it that is all made out of metal. All of it is built into one solid unit that is securely bolted into the wall. Above the sink is an 8 by 12 inch metal plate that is meant to serve as a mirror. Get used to a blurred "you" reflecting back whenever you shave while you are here is all that I can offer if you use it.

Behind me on the wall to my left is a metal bunk with a green 4 inch thick plastic mattress laying on top of it. There is a plastic pillow on it as well. A set of sheets and towels will be given to me at some point. Along the other wall from the bed is a simple metal table with a single metal chair that has been welded to the base of it. The desk and flat table back are all bolted on the wall together. There are two metal hooks for my towels or clothes to be hung from that are opposite the toilet just by my door at shoulder level.

Along the back wall are two windows. Don't bother, I already checked them out. Cannot see shit.

The screen wire mesh outside is so thick over the glass, that combined with the metal screens built into the window frame from the inside of the glass as well, makes it all impossible to see much.

It's all feeling like when you see the film images in a science fiction movie where they emulate the inside of a fly's eye...you really have to see the skyline of a city through this metal mesh to appreciate what it was like. Waste of fucking time looking outside and a headache trying to see anything inside.

As I looked out of my cell through one of the upright cuts in my metal door, I could see that I am in a squared pod of cells. Mostly all of it is made of the same cinder blocks and wire mesh and all painted the same "Robins-egg blue" that is the same as my cell color. There are 7 other cells on my pod and one semi-open area with a plastic curtain hung across it. A set of metal bars can be slid across this I see, so this is the "shower room". The bars are set up to seal it like a cell and it was remotely opened from within the control room. I can see that this must be serving as the shower room for all of the men on the lone pod whom I shared cells with.

In the center of the pod is a caged area with a shiny metal picnic table side bolted to the floor. 4 metal seats all bolted to the floor surround this table.

There is a gray metal door sealing this area from the cells which men would be let in through I see. There is a blue plastic phone bolted to the day-room wire mesh wall off in a corner of this cage.

Outside of the mesh day-room there is a metal door on either end of this pod allowing the guards to enter from the door right next to the "shower" to my left, or from the other end of the last cell which is to my right. My cell was right in the middle of the pod so I could see all but the two corner cells to my flat left or right. I could clearly see who was in the other cells if the men were to stand at their door when I was as well.

It is not like I had to stand at my door to be heard. With each pod of cells only spread about by about 25 feet apart, you felt like you are in a connected unit where each man can be in your conversation instantly. Your ability to blot out the others would only be a set of headphones or sleep. Otherwise this was very up close and personal. You shared each sneeze, every cough, and nearly every word was free game.

That lone telephone that was bolted to the wall in the day-room was your only instant communication outside. It was on this lone line of communication which all 8 men on the pod would use to call the outside world via collect calls. All calls were recorded and listened to by the staff.

This pod which was called "C" Pod was now my home. It was one of three pods that faced the North side of this building. In the center section between the North and South sides of the unit was a laughable area called the "outside exercise area". Out there, 4 cages were set up that were 5 feet wide and 12 feet long. Literally long enough to do a silly jog that ended each way with a short turn to come back. Basically 4 dog kennels wrapped in so much wire, that you literally could not see direct sunlight on a sunny day.

No one got onto the top floor unless the guards at the top allowed the elevator to come up there by use of security keys.

There was only one way in and one way out except for always locked stairs attached to the outside. I had just come up on this creaking, horribly slow and shaky elevator, while 2 enormous prison officers were crowding me against the back wall with their clubs holding me against the wall. The whole thing was so small that I soon felt like I was on the cusp of feeling smothered inside of a 5 foot by 5 foot squared box.

When I walked to my pod on the arms of my escorts I was stopped by the administration waiting there first. There were about 12 in all. "White Shirts and Shot-callers" we referred to them as being. The folks what decided where and when and what you got.

Right in front of the guards that were holding me, they read out what I was convicted of, when I was sentenced to die, and then which pod these guards were to take me into. It was right at this point that I learned that I was under psychiatric care as I was deemed too mentally disturbed to be sent to SCI-Greene County prison. I was informed on the spot that due to my violence previously inside prison, (and how I was convicted of a mentally deranged crime), that I was unfit to be trusted out of my cell.

Further, that due to my previous escape that, I was also a risk to the orderly function of a normal Death Row unit. I was offered medications then and the whole time I stood mute to it all.

The staff concluded my "welcome" to the unit by informing me that as I was now under psychiatric detention, while further that I was now also subject to the rules and regulations of the mental health division. I had no clue what any of this was to mean at first. I just had a floor filled with male and female staff just announce what a mentally fucked up person that I was, and how since I was deemed such a nutcase, that I was not to be trusted in an open setting. I had a fly in my mind pictured on the wall behind them all that held my focus.

When you have something this ugly hanging over you, you do not quip one line jokes. You own the humiliation of the moment whether guilty or not, because you are being held up to the light that no one seems to handle. That sucked.

Just as I was taken out of my chains and stripped down one last time to be naked for being searched before I was put finally into my cell, I knew that each man who was to fill the other cells would be put through this same routine as well. It was going to make them feel just as shitty too I bet.

I did not know it at the time that I focused on all of that initiation process, but as each man was brought into my pod after me, I soon learned further that I was going to be set up to be part of one of the sickest experiments ever imagined.

The guards who would be assigned to this unit were led by a staff Sergeant. Unfortunately for us all, he was a Rage-aholic of a man who's diminutive figure at only 5 foot 6 inches tall, was mated to a huge ego. His level of outbursts and uncontrolled venomous acts would be on show right away to any who slighted him.

My first confrontation with the man who ran day to day operations on all 6 pods was ugly.

He stood in front of my cell and read out the newspaper accounts of my case which he had printed out on white sheets of paper. His version of my incarceration was punctuated with lots of nasty comments and such, but for the record, here is what he made sure to let me know that he knew about me.

The story Goes:

Linda Mae Craig was working in the Tri-State Mall located in the state of Delaware back in December of 1981. As she left work at 4:pm on December 15th 1981 Police said that I ran or walked up to her and punched her in the face as she got into her car, thus breaking her teeth. They said I then dragged her out of her shoes (which were found there the next morning where her car was). They said I put Mrs. Craig into her own car and then drove away with her into Pennsylvania, located only some 3 miles away.

Police said that I then cut away Mrs. Craig's clothes with a knife and that I raped her. The police claim I stabbed Mrs. Craig brutally six times in the chest with the same knife, and that I dumped her dying body in the parking lot of a Church where the rape took place.

Police said that I then drove Mrs. Craig's own car right past her home and left it along the side of the road near her house with the engine running, car doors locked , along with the interior lights left on inside...The authorities claimed I "staged the interior of the car" complete with my leaving behind the bloody gloves worn during the crime, as a taunt to the police upon finding this all.

My presenter then went on to highlight my escape in 1985, along with all of the infractions on my records within the department of corrections. It was all summed up nicely when he leaned forward and told me how much "fuckin' fun he was going to have with a sick piece of shit like me". That was 5 minutes after I got placed into my cell.

What made me "special" to this man was that the authorities said that I did my crimes because I was mentally sick and twisted. They say that for weeks I had stalked Mrs. Craig and that I planned her murder in a psychotically driven scheme.

The authorities said that because I was deranged and on drugs, (that I had a mentally malfunctioning brain anyway), that I killed Mrs. Craig because I had a girlfriend of 3 weeks break my heart. That was a moment of real laughter for my pal reading all of this out for me.

The fact that I shared B+ blood which was the same as the evidence found at the scene pf the crime, all made it so easy to convict me. It was a valid reason for this man to mock me as well. My life in prison before this man had been brutal enough, but now I was being reminded all over of what a piece of shit I was in his eyes and he was going to used to hurt me further.

I was sent to Death Row after a fast, 3 day long murder trial. Then only following 4 hours of jury deliberations were spent deciding my punishment in 1982, I was then sentence to die in the State's electric chair. I was 21 years old.

I was angry and people were constantly taking shots at me inside of jail physically. I went to my first State prison and assaulted an officer during a fight with another inmate only 2 months into my stay there. That assault was used by the Governor, (along with an escape attempt in 1981 of another Death Row guy named John Lesko which had nothing to do with me), to then lock every guy down in solitary confinement in Pennsylvania. I was so hated by every man who blamed me for them being in solitary confinement, that I was shunned by all who occupied cells around me on Death Row initially.

Sgt. Rage made it clear that I was there before him to now answer for all of my misdeeds like this, and for any others which he could think of.

I really did not like how I was in a sealed unit with a man who could do virtually anything he wished to me, so I kept quiet throughout his whole performance.

As I stood before that door listening to him belittle me, I had a total of 105 years on top of my actual sentence of Death, so I was never meant to *ever* get out alive. If I was not executed, the number of years to be serve by me would be my fate any way. This man knew this and so did I at the time. He just had to point it out to me rudely to make me feel as low as possible. Never in his wildest dreams could he ever imagine I would get out one day and tell of this story.

There was one other prisoner already on this new pod of mine when I had gotten put into my cell. I could not see them, but I saw a shadow moving inside of the cell when they walked towards their door. I waited without talking for what was to come next.

Having this faceless man listen to my history and having the same thing probably done to them by the Sergeant made neither one of us want to speak. I learned that it is bad form to be the first one to speak when put into a new setting anyway, but this was some new shit I never faced before. This guy was making a point of playing with each guy coming into the pod, or I was just one of the few whom he was going to toy with. Either way it really did not matter because I was screwed.

When you are placed in control of someone mentally distorted it makes you seem fearful and alone, or you have a vulnerable sense to know you are on a "list". It is daunting to think that this guy has so much power that he can let 3 guys out of their cells in the day-room who are all armed. They attack you are done. He can push one button to open a cell from the control booth and your life is over. I knew from that first moment that I had to tread very carefully with this man.

Nick Yarris

2. EVERY KIND OF CRAZY

Ten minutes after I was put in my new cell I heard all the sounds of the guards bringing in a new guy to the pod. In short order the sliding metal and glass doors leading to the outside hallway popped open. From my cell door-crack I saw bodies moving as they walked our way, past the central control unit. I stood at my door watching as the door slid open to the pod. Then 2 officers brought in the next man. "Damn" I said under my breath, "not *him*"...

The very first guy I was going to have to be on this pod with was none other than Roland. I am so loathed to be sharing this creature's tale at all.

Standing at about 5 foot 8 *maybe* on a good day of his life, and weighing about 135 pounds to 140 pounds? Yeah, that is about right. Roland is a black guy who has a shaved head and speaks with a lisp. He was medium complexioned of skin tone. His voice is somewhere between effeminate and menacing. He is a chameleon. This dude is so good at fooling people that I have to always remember who he is. I also always remember what our personal history is.

There has always been hate between us.

Now, the rules are simple on Death Row: If you want everyone to leave you alone, you deal with your enemies by yourself. If you tip off the guards, or make them know that you got someone after you, everyone lines up together to get your ass back for being a "rat". So, hate him or not, this sicko was my new housemate of sorts. I was going to have to be very careful with him being so close by without saying a word to anyone about our feud.

Who is Roland? Sergeant Rage made a real go of telling it all when the guards got him into his cell. He are the facts.

Roland was living in Pittsburgh at the time of his arrest in the late 1980's for minor felony crimes. His path to Death Row is as sick as anyone can imagine. In 1988 Roland kidnapped 3 women in their late 80's and beat them to death with his bare hands. His nickname in the newspaper was "The Karate Killer".

Yes, this lame and evil twisted psycho went to jail and learned martial arts early on. He then got out of jail to use this attacking style on his victims later on. A lot of what happened has been pretty much kept from the news papers or is not widely known outside of law books and prison records.

Unfortunately for Roland though, Sergeant Rage was working here in Pittsburgh when it all took place.

Roland was in custody and serving time for a series of crimes that had him in the local Pittsburgh county jail located about 5 miles from the state prison. Mostly burglary or robbery. He was locked up in a place named the Washington County Pa. Jail awaiting trial for all of this. While he was there, an inmate escaped custody and had badly embarrassed the authorities. Roland used this incident as a ploy to get himself out of jail.

Roland is completely able to immerse himself in anything that he says about himself, so he went to the authorities claiming that he could help the FBI find the local escapee named William Wallace. Believe it or not, the FBI went right along with it.

Sergeant Rage said he was shocked that Roland somehow used his maniacal charms on some dimwit FBI agent, and then convinced them that if they let him out of jail, how he could go and find Wallace.

Roland was in no way *not* going to take this freedom from custody as him then actually acting like he himself was an FBI agent. He went out and put on a suit and tie began going around Pittsburgh trying to catch this man whom he claimed that he knew the location of.

At first Roland robbed locals who were small time drug dealers, all while claiming at first that he was an FBI agent.

He beat a young woman with a bottle in front of her 3 year old child when she had "refused" to give up the information which he sought from her about William Wallace. The woman never even knew this man named Wallace and had only met Roland at a bus stop in the area ten minutes before he savagely beat her.

But all of this hunting for someone he probably did not even know soon got boring for Roland, as he was tiring of looking for someone with no chance of actually finding them. Well, since he did not have wheels, Roland tried to first abduct a woman in her 40's who was sitting alone in a parking lot. Roland tried to convince her that someone had messed with her car tire. She was able deflect his attempt to do anything to her, and she went to the police and reported the incident soon afterwards.

An hour after trying to abduct the first woman, Roland went up to an 88 year old lady who was just getting into her car at a mall. He then conned her into thinking she had car trouble with her rear tire, all just as he had before with the younger woman.

Roland then got the 88 year old lady into her own car by convincing her that he was going to care for everything broken or wrong. Roland then got behind the wheel and he drove her over to another part of this big parking lot area of a mall.

It was there that he also picked up two friends of this lady who were just at lunch with her, and conned them into joining them in the same car. Her friends, who were both 86 and 81 years old respectively, all went passively along with Roland as they drive off.

Then, with Roland driving them all together in the car belonging to the 88 year old, he took them into some woods nearby in area located just outside of Pittsburgh.

He got them out of the car one by one. He stood them against some trees and then he began to beat all three of them to death with his bare hands.

Roland made sport of his victims in how he broke each one of the three women's legs first. He made sure none could escape his terror. He delighted in making them suffer as he went to work on them with spinning kicks or Karate blows to their necks and faces. He practiced his elbow blows on one woman's face 11 times. He took trinkets from each victim as he beat on them, ripping earrings out while stomping a victim.

Shattering one woman's hip while standing on her, Roland even danced about in joy on them as a trampoline...

This horrific crime was so unbelievable, and was one of the worst cases of the FBI allowing a man out of jail only to commit murders, that everyone wanted this thing to quickly go away.

It was like this was all a bad nightmare that they all wanted to hurry through so they could forget. This is why it never got national news attention in America. It was why Sergeant Rage said Roland needed to die badly for his crimes.

I cringed as Sergeant Rage went on and on...

He concentrated on how low Roland was for some of the twisted acts he did, reading in detail:

In what was described by the coroner as "prolonged effort to inflict as much pain as possible on the victims"...these 3 poor old ladies were subjected to the sickest imaginable deaths anyone could conjure up. They say that it took an hour for Roland Roland to beat all three old women to death, only because he made so much sport of it. He harmed them enough to allow them to crawl on the ground in a feeble attempt to flee as he sat on them and laughed.

He mocked them as they plead for their lives too, while all along he finished them off one at a time, until he had slowly murdered all three in the most pitiless way he could.

That was a nasty moment. But the presenter of Roland's sins soon cheered up while pointing out things like:

The jury was so angry in how they wanted this nightmare over as fast as humanly possible. They convicted Roland of first degree murder in just 20 minutes.

Now I know from the simple process involved that it usually takes them about 15 minutes just to sign the fully completed set of verdict slips, a process in which each juror is asked to write their names on sheets of paper next each count facing the man who is on trial. So basically what this means is that Roland was convicted the moment he sat his sick ass in the defendant's chair at the start of the trail.

But back on the day of his crime, what he did after this creature of a man had used all sorts of dirty tricks to break these woman's limbs and bodies was not even *close* to showing how truly sick he is. What he did is so unbelievable that it blows my mind every time I think of Sergeant Rage going into it all.

You see, Roland went to a fuel station nearby to the murders directly after killing these three old people in the woods like a savage beast who was toying with his prey.

Roland was calmly driving the victim's car who owned it, and parked right next to the pumps. He had his smile on his face people said and he seemed super relaxed witnesses also say. Such a pleasant smile for all whom he met really.

And just as calmly as a man coming from church in a nice suit and tie, he then interacted with everyone whom he met inside of the station's shop after filling his car with fuel.

Roland walked around serenely and picked out a cold soda and began drinking it as he walked around the store looking at items.

The woman who worked there said he hummed a little tune as he quenched his thirst like it was just a long day outside. Roland paused only once during his time inside the shop. The woman inside who worked there was made nervous when she said Roland "reacted" to a little girl who had just then walked into the shop with her mother. She was coming into the shop along with her mother who was holding her hand when Roland soon changed from serene to furtive and on edge.

The shop keeper said she noticed Roland went behind the potato chip stand and kind of hunched over and looked through the items as if not to be seen by the woman. She at first thought he was not wanting to be recognized by an ex girlfriend, and did not put much more into it.

Then as the little girl went past Roland with her mother, She saw Roland reaching into his pocket. She said he went after the girl and put his hand on her shoulder and turned her around to face Roland who had then knelt down.

Roland smiled at this little girl lovingly. He asked her what her name was and he said she was a "special" little girl. The mother of the girl came over and stood nervously by her child wanting to hear what was going on.

Roland then he reached into his pocket and he took out a gift for her child he said. Roland was so passive and soft toned as he did all this that the mother never questioned why a stranger would want to give her child any thing.

Roland opened his hand. He gave this small child a gold chain which had a locket on it that was in his hand. He told her to take it and keep it until she was "older".

When the mother of this little girl stepped over to take the necklace in her hands to see it, Roland got all nervous and agitated, so she backed away and Roland told the little girl how he had to go then.

When the little girl looked down and saw the gold chain in her hand she smiled up at this man who seemed to want her to have this present.

Roland then told the child's mother as they walked away awkwardly that it was okay, and that he was wealthy. He said that he enjoyed passing out gifts to strangers. They hurried to the door after Roland began stroking the little girls' face lovingly.

The mother acted all skittish they say but Roland merrily walked out of the shop still humming his tune...Of course we all know that the necklace belonged to one of the murdered women.

Roland then drove only a half a mile away from the fuel station and there he broke into an elderly lady's home. Just ten minutes after he was in the station with the child, there he was next, stealing some items from some lady's house located right near the fuel station.

Now the items taken were very odd. Items including a lady's dress, a set of hosiery, a blonde wig that was from a party costume, along with a pair of lady's shoes.

Just 45 minutes after Roland had been in the fuel station handing out trophies of his kills from one of the dead women whom he had just murdered, he drove back past the very same fuel station a second time. This time he even waived to the attendant outside who noted that this car with Roland driving it was coming from the opposite direction which he first went past. Roland was obviously coming from this burglary of the old lady's home, and was now going back to where he first came from killing the 3 women in the woods...

Evidence at trial showed that Roland went back to the crime scene a second time. It was there that he then dressed up as an old woman in his stolen items from the burglary. What he did to those women in the woods only God knows.

Apparently he spent a prolonged time with all three of his dead elderly victims, all while himself dressed as one. He reposed their dead bodies. He even did some more damage to one of the corpses which had fallen over from being propped up by Roland. Evidence showed Roland had been kicking this human body over 40 times after they were dead. The indentations of a woman's shoe that was pointed in the front, all fit exactly into the pattern of abuse on the corpse.

Roland then masturbated over his victims and left the scene of his butchery after he spent his time playing with the women. Then of course, he went down that same lane it all took place on, driving back to the fuel station a third time.

This time he was not the suave man in a nice suit who was so calm and sweet while handing out gold necklaces. This time he was in a panic as the car's engine had cut off and he seemed terrified to not be able to drive it. It actually coasted without engine power into the station forecourt.

Gone was the smooth effort to be calm, Roland was near to tears of panic when he thought the car was not operable and he was stuck there.

A mechanic who worked in the station helped him re-start the car after several tries.

The mechanic claimed that he thought later that he might have seen a pair of "messed up" women's shoes in the back of the car trunk area, but he claimed that Roland closed it up before he could see more.

Sergeant Rage said that there would be no shoes like that on this unit and that Roland was not allowed any wigs either with a lot of mirth to his comment. Why did I hate this monster Roland?

This was the type of monster who actually lived completely in denial of his acts. In jail this predator actually went around like he was such a nice guy to those whom he wanted to suck up to, all while he was constantly preying on any young guys sexually. He had a habit of breaking down young guys to lure them into sex with trickery and there were many who came to prison at the same time whom he also tried all sorts of devious shit on.

What made me sick to my stomach was how he paid for pediatric magazines so that he could look at small children and masturbate to it. He did this back in my last prison which we were together in. He knew enough that child porn was illegal and never allowed in prison. Somehow he knew that he could get these innocent pediatrician publications sent into prison instead.

Roland knew that he could see children in these magazines naked or half naked, and that was enough for him to masturbate over in his cleverly sick way.

It was these magazines that made *me* have to be the one to beat his ass in our last prison stay together as well.

I will keep this brief, as it is just why Roland and I were always going to have to do a sick "dance" together, the one with him trying to murder me over this incident.

The guard handing out mail saw the child pediatric care mags in the pile of mail that he held one day while on my old prison Block. The man got angry at this sicko receiving them so he decided Roland needed to be brought down a peg. This guard also hated me unfortunately, as he had a personal dislike of me for my escape from that prison in 1985, so it was easy for him to pick my sorry ass out to do his bidding.

So, one Sunday in August of 1992 when there was no Lieutenant on B-Block, the guards on shift put me and Roland together in an exercise cage located outside of the rear of B-Block. This was used as a set up for us to entertain the guards in a good ol' fight.

Instead of me fighting Bruce Lee and his Karate moves, I was dealing with a guy clinging to me desperately, one who scratched me and bit me, all while I did my best to crack his jaw with my fists.

All that"Karate" that Roland claimed that knew was bullshit when it comes to physical brawling, especially if it is jail-house made up Karate which you were taught by some other inmate.

At 6 foot 2 and 225 pounds, I was far more superior to him physically at my age of 30 years old when we fought.

I made his mouth mush with my fists and he left a set of scars on my face just below my right eye from deep gouges he made with his nails that are still there today on my face.

That is why, as soon as I saw that Roland was being put in the cell that was located only three doors away from my own, that this shit was not over with. With Sergeant Rage running this show it was about to get real dicey for us both Roland.

When the guards left the pod, Roland came to his cell door and looked at me through the door of his cell as I stood at my door. I snorted in disgust that we had to be so close to one another, being only 15 feet apart. When he recognized me he laughed his sick little mocking chuckle at me. We both knew what time it was for us and neither one of us was going to say anything to the "po-po" about it. We both nodded at the same time, like a signal to us each that is was game on. Roland then went silent.

A short while later, and here comes the next guy being brought in by guards. I silently prayed it was not one of the "shit tossers" being put on our pod. I hate being around the guys who have lost their minds. They throw urine or shit out of their cells all the time. It is horrible to live around the insane while in prison.

What followed next made my heart sink. It was someone I actually cared for. Keith.

I knew Keith from Huntingdon prison as well. He was there before me when I first got to Death Row back in 1983. Keith was white and he stood about 6 foot 1 and weighed about 175 pounds. He had sandy blond hair that was thinning and he wore eyeglasses too. He was in agony physically as his hip had been shattered by being shoved down a flight of metal stairs by a guard some years back.

Keith was handcuffed at the time that he fell and could not brace himself, so he ended up shattering his right hip during the fall. He screamed and passed out soon afterwards. I was shoved back into my cell right then because I was standing right behind prison guard on the day that he did this to Keith. He kicked Keith in the small of his back and sent him flying down the steps. He thought it was a riot and laughed his ass off. He only stopped laughing when Keith screamed for way too long from being injured.

What a pitiful sight to see Keith hobbling along slowly with the guards pulling him. His glasses were steamed up and his hair was matted with sweat from the effort to get over to his cell that was next to mine on my left. I called out; "You okay Keith"? He answered back "Yeah Nick".

Crippled or not, he too got stripped and ass searched like me.

With Keith right in the cell next to me, I could hear his painful groans though the mesh vent that connected our cells. I knelt down and I could see his feet through the mesh as well.

When the guards left, I spoke to Keith through the vents and told him who it is that I saw in the other cell across from us. I also said that I had no idea who was in the cell that had an inmate in it already.

Keith had to go to the toilet he said, so I left him then to go back to the door and see who else we had to live with here on this pod.

It sucked when he had his case read out by Sergeant Rage next. I really will do it justice for how it should be told and ignore how he made it all out to be.

My friend Keith...shit, I have no other way to describe him... I loved the guy in some ways, so yeah he was my friend. He was kind and gentle and actually funny to talk to at times. He had a wicked laugh and I don't know what else to say other than he was a nice guy who had killed his best friend.

Keith grew up in a rural part of Pennsylvania and he started doing burglaries with his childhood friend. Now, this guy he shot is someone who grew up with Keith, had sleep overs with Keith as a boy, and shared many days at their respective houses together as children.

But when Keith and his friend got caught, Keith's friend informed on him to serve less time and Keith took it very personally.

Keith lured his friend to a river one night and shot him point blank in the back of his head. As Keith then climbed the bank of the river, a police officer appeared just then. He knew Keith from the area and asked what he was doing. Keith said "I was shooting some rats". That one line became the headlines at his trial.

Well, being caught red handed while shooting your childhood friend in the head, all because he was going to be a witness against you, was a short trip to Death Row for Keith. Sergeant Rage said he was sure not to expect a birthday card from his friends if Keith shot them all in the head like that.

I saw this man Keith pay over and over for what he did to his friend by the hands of some of the sickest guards in Huntingdon. I saw him suffer his own anguish over what he did whenever we spoke.

Once the guard broke his hip, Keith suffered in pain like no one else whom I ever saw before handle. The way he accepted his punishment and never once acted proud of what he did made me respect him. Some humans actually show remorse for years in ways we never get to see. I saw it all from this man.

While I was thinking of Keith and all of that, I swear that when I saw who was being brought along the corridor to our cell pod next, I half blurted out to Keith; 'Oh God, not *this* idiot'!

Rump came next. Great jailhouse name for this guy.

Ronnie is his actual name. And right to my immediate dislike, I saw how he was being put in the cell right next to me on my right side. Great, 'now this guy will be on the door talking, or always speaking to me directly in my connecting air vents all day', I thought to myself. It was not even before the guards had finished taking his cuffs off that he was calling out; "Hey Buddy" to Roland, and then talking about how shitty the ride over in the prison bus was for us all, and then how he was hungry already.

In other words, Rump was a life long *inmate* who's only complaints or thoughts were going to be prison related. Literally mentally retarded.

Lets go down his "little path of really dark shit" as Sergeant Rage said about Rump.

"Rump", (and yes he really likes it when others call him this name), has an IQ of 81. I know this because he boasted that he "beat" being labeled retarded previously, only because of his actual score. He proudly told us all one day that you have to have an IQ of 80 or less to be considered **really** retarded.

Ronnie was white and he stood about 5 foot 10 and was an easy 200 pounds. He had "Cave-man" like features of a low sloping forehead with close set eyes, completed with thick greasy brown hair.

His hair was always combed into a pompadour style from the 60's. He is very coarse and obtuse in speaking terms. Ronnie is a pain in the ass to live next to because he is just so fucking stupid.

Other than my turn of having my tale told, Sergeant Rage really had fun broadcasting about Ronnie.

Rump grew up in a rural part of Pennsylvania with 8 other children for siblings. His mother was an abusive alcoholic and his father even at times locked Ronnie in a dog kennel that was filled with human or dog feces. He had to endure days of physical and mental abuse for being mentally "slow".

Rump was even made to eat garbage to survive until he began running away and living in the woods. At age 12 he lived in the abandoned cars or trucks left in woods near his hometown, becoming as feral a creature that any human would. He was soon in and out of jail constantly for petty crimes until the age of 18. This man had one of the sickest documented childhoods ever recorded until then the news papers reported.

In 1974 Rump was convicted of a brutal rape of a woman whom he attacked after hiding in the men's room of a bar late one night awaiting for it to close. The physical abuse done to the victim was horrendous and Rump was given 15 years for this first criminal conviction this serious in nature. He would serve every day of his sentence without once being granted early release. He was too violent to ever be considered they said.

So, after he finished his maximum days of sentence in 1989 for his rape conviction, he went right back to the same bar and waited until it closed. This time he tortured and then murdered the bar keeper in the same place where it all began and he stayed to have drinks afterwards.

At age 56 or so when he stood before me in Pittsburgh Penitentiary , he had been in prison or juvenile detention for 40 or more of those 56 years he had lived.

Rump was severely institutionalized and he was someone who would kill you without hesitation for the slightest insult. I used a lot of charm to stay ahead of Rump and keep him at bay because he is that pit bull who hangs from a tree branch and wags his tail if you hit him with a stick because his teeth are sunk into any thing moving.

Sergeant Rage said that he was never going to let Ronnie buy drinks for him in a bar and yet Rump seemed not so hurt by this comment.

Next through the door came Bobby. Another one you had to watch out for because he was a big nasty biker type. Bobby weighed in at over 300 lbs. He was well over 6 foot 2 as well, so he was a lump of a human being. This guy was mean as fuck to deal with. He had black hair and black eyes to match.

Bobby wore a beard that was long and his hair was long and greasy too. Remarkably though, he had very white skin, like at some point you could see that he was a nice looking teenage boy. That was long gone now though.

Ol' Bobby had a nasty habit of concocting all sorts of clever weapons to try and kill other prisoners with in the past, Sergeant Rage said he like Bobby for this.

I saw this bastard do some clever and devious things and I wanted no parts of Bobby. We had a mutual "non-feelings" kind of relationship for one another. He would go along with anything done to me, but he himself would not take me on directly as we had no beef between us which he could claim for motivation.

Bobby played by the rules mostly, so we could have this weird relationship where if it came down to it, he would only act if I became a threat or if I somehow crossed him.

Only problem was, Bobby had severe schizophrenia and frontal lobe damage done to him from the calcification of his brain. This was made worse by his years of using Methamphetamine. It did not take much for him to "think" someone was talking shit behind his back for Bobby to then try and kill this person for it.

His news paper clippings were unpleasant.

The real version read out to us pales to what this man tells others, so I gotta tell you what you would hear vs what is truth if you let Bobby tell it.

See, I was standing in the individual cage that I was exercising in back in Huntingdon when Bobby told his version of his "pedigree" to another pair of wanna be bikers standing in the cages that were next to his.

They were new to Death Row and he was putting on a front for them.

Bobby starting telling these guys how this one time, how this "Dude" had ripped him off. He then said how he and two of his "soldiers" from his gang went over to dole out some justice for this punk over this debt.

I was working out in my own cage then and acted like it was nothing to do with me as Bobby went on with his version of things.

According to Bobby on that day when I heard him telling tales in the cages, this "Dude" was a real bad-ass, and he had a reputation for all sorts of violence. He went into detail about how big and menacing this guy was, but he quickly added how Bobby liked that kind of thing, because Bobby was a self described "Beast".

Then his story got juicier as he told them how he burst in on the guy with some hooker sucking his dick in bed. He then told how they trashed the place before Bobby got down to work torturing the guy. He said he had to, it was for the combination to his safe which they found in the place. (Bobby did a side-step of how they killed the girl in this telling I later noted) He went on to get all upbeat on the big finish to his story with the loads of cash and drugs that they got from this "Dude" in the robbery. Sgt. Rage told a different tale.

According to police, Bobby at age 25 was already ravaged by schizophrenia. He convinced two friends of his to do a burglary. None of them were on motorcycles roaring over there as a gang during this event. They drove over in Bobby's mothers car. It was she whom he was living in the basement of doing while shooting Methamphetamine all day. He had a broken down motorcycle half in parts sitting in the front garden.

The group led by Bobby that day drove around getting high and started looking for ways to get money. When they found an apartment which they thought no one was inside of, they broke in to steal items. They found a man and his 19 year old girlfriend inside of the apartment asleep. This kind of crime was rare back then. Bobby and his two pals went to work on the victims sadistically in that apartment upon finding them.

First they took silver duct tape and completely covered booth victim's faces. save for nose holes and eye holes. Then then wrapped electrical chords around their necks and began torturing them and choking them police said.

Eventually, after toying with the man for nearly 40 minutes, Bobby stabbed him repeatedly and strangled him for good measure at the kitchen table, all as his 19 year old girlfriend watched on in horror. He then drug the 19 year old girl downstairs to the basement.

Bobby beat her with a wrench so hard it was embedded in her head. Bobby then he stabbed her repeatedly and left her curled up on the basement floor. He and his 2 pals partied in the apartment with the victims still there until leaving the next morning.

Bobby was convicted and several inmates even testified at trial as to the many times Bobby openly told them about the crime in made up form. He was unflinching as he was handed his death sentence and never once showed any emotion. Why would he?

In his reality, Bobby took on a rival biker gang and he had all this other made up reality that he was clinging to in his head.

Now, all you had to do to get yourself murdered by Bobby "the Beast" was to laugh at the wrong thing or at the wrong time. Once he wanted you dead for some paranoid thought that came to him, that was all he talked of, thought of, or worked at getting done.

This guy is so huge and so menacing that many of the staff were intimidated by his aggression. I stayed well clear of Bobby on a good day. I saw that he was always looking at you suspiciously, as if you were thinking of doing him wrong somehow. Very eerie to be around a mentally ill person who can squash you with his giant frame.

Shame of it is, nearly 80 per cent of all Death Row men have some form of mental illness or brain disease. The ones with a disorder can be dealt with. The ones like Bobby who have non treatable schizophrenia, are the ones who are capable of the most bizarre behavior at any moment.

Of all the acts of anyone I witnessed, one thing Bobby was soon to do on this pod will never leave me. It makes me sick at times to recall even. The fact that a guard let him do it and laughed over it is what makes it all the more worse.

After Bobby went into his cell, they brought us Dave. Dave is a white guy that stood about 5 foot 10 and he had a big ol' gut on him from sitting around eating snacks all day. An easy 250 pounds of fatty Dave was near to 50 years old when he was in the unit right then. Silvering hair in a short, close cropped haircut that was reminiscent of the 1960's hair style, Dave was also from rural Pennsylvania. He was an odd sort. He actually just got put back on Death Row for a 3rd time for the same murder, as he entered this place.

Sgt. Rage clearly did not like Dave and he loved sharing how Dave got convicted first in 1986 of murdering a handicapped child while stealing the donations given to the child at a charity event.

This was an event which Dave and his brother had attended that same day no less.

Dave broke into the home with his brother in tow that same night, and they then ransacked the house for the money meant for the disabled child.

When they found out that the child had awakened during the crime, Dave butchered the little handicapped boy who would have never been able to identify them anyway.

On appeal there was a technical error. Dave got sentenced to death by a second jury during his second trial. On Appeal they again reversed his conviction for faulty instructions to the jury.

So then they gave him a 3rd jury trial.

Well after 36 jurors later, and 3 times of his brother going into court and telling them the same story of how Dave killed the handicapped child for money to buy drugs and whores, well then you become "Bad Luck Dave" on Death Row.

Sergeant Rage said that of all the men whom he had to put in a cell that day, how Dave was by far the one whom he wanted executed first.

I had only spent brief times with Dave because of all the back and forth to court he took trips on so much that I barely knew him. I had no issues with him other than one. He thought he was a bit able to judge me for a sex crime after he had butchered a handicapped child, but lets not quibble about the details Dave...

Dave was not the brightest guy and he was for some reason really good buddies with Bobby. It was like Dave was a minion to Bobby and together these two butchers had an ersatz homosexual relationship wherein Dave thrived off of every witty thing that Bobby had to offer out of his mouth.

The guards put Dave right next to Bobby in the cell second from the end of course.

No sooner was Dave out of his cuffs and in that cell did he and Bobby disappear into the vents for a lovely catch up chat. I bet they were all aflutter for the one hour that they were just apart downstairs, you know, since both were on a prison bus together on their way here all day.

Yes, they sat next to one another on the bus as well and were quietly chatting the whole time, like some old married couple. I did not have to hear the two of them speaking to know what they were saying.

As a partnered pair, they were already chattering about who the guards were putting in the cells around "them" and who "they" were going to have to be dealing with on the pod.

I swear, it is so weird to see men do this thing where they feel like they are married to some guy who they never even knew before prison.

At this point I was just hoping that whomever went into the last two cells were not some of the men that was on the "hit list" of any of these guys whom I was already locked up on the pod with. This was a place that no one was getting a chance to be left alone inside of from this kind of bad blood closeness. This "pod" vs the old style of prison wherein everyone faces one direction was going to make this a fish bowl full. One full of sharks looking to prey. No way this is not going to be a frenzy I told myself. Just then, pop goes the door and we hear them coming with our new latest chum.

The next man did not walk into the pod. He was rolled into the unit in his wheelchair. George.

Oh man, if there ever was a case for "worst life ever argument", this is the guy who wins it hands down.

George used to stand upright at about 5 foot 6 inches tall. He has bright orange hair and freckles. He is obese and he has terrible acne scars. A white guy in his early 30's that looked like he had dementia.

I never saw fingernails that long, nor that filthy on a human before him. He was a retched mess. I was not there, but story is that George went to court on appeal walking like a normal person after his trial. He came back in a wheel chair to Death Row.

Rumor was that they sodomized him with a riot club and damaged his internal organs while they broke some bones in his back too. Story George tells you don't make sense as he has said many stories over time. All I knew was that he was crippled now, and he was one of the saddest cases ever before that happened. Here is how poor George-Boy got there according to Sergeant Rage and his news clippings collection:

According to police George was convicted of murdering his girlfriend in 1987. He was eating her flesh when he was caught red-handed by police they say.

Yes, George was literally still lying on top of his victim and still cannibalizing her as the police dragged him off of her.

George had been drinking and doing drugs with his girlfriend in 1987 when they had an argument. George began violently assaulting his girlfriend. Her screams were heard by many in a small community in Eastern Pennsylvania where they both lived. As the fight went into a serious attack behind a bar in an alley strewn with garbage, police were called to the scene.

When they got there, George was sitting astride his now dead girlfriend and he was eating her breasts. By the time they pulled him off, he had eaten an entire breast and most of the second one. The police were ill instantly at the sight of what he did to his victim. George don't tell his story to anyone, he just did whatever he could to drink prison "hooch" or take pills to blot out what he did once.

George was probably the most docile *sober* person whom I have ever met. Meek beyond meek, he was obviously diminished mentally. This, on top of the many years of abuse in and out of prison that he was subjected to, meant that he was ruined as human is how I can describe it. George was so easy to manipulate that others often sexually abused him or took whatever possessions, and or money that he had sent in to him from outside. Why was he like this?

George was raised in a house where his mother was ultra Christian. She was religiosity driven to change George from evil spirits that she thought made him slow minded. She made George kneel on shards of broken glass and read the bible for hours each day when she found he had wet his bed at night.

His father beat him with a metal rod from a fence that had tape on the handle for a good grip. George was made to drink his own piss to survive after being left in a box for days when he broke rules.

At age of just 14 authorities said George was so messed up mentally from this type of abuse that he ate a pet cat while it was still alive. He was sitting with this pet he had been playing with in front of a neighbors home. He was high on glue which he had been inhaling in front of the home for hours. He told people he did not remember any of it.

The only reason that George did not get mental health treatment and be put away for life, or even be spared the death penalty was all due to the local prosecutor of the time who handled his case. He wanted the "Cannibal" case to be bigger than some mentally destroyed human out of their head on booze. No, that would not serve any career moves!

So, they took the most pitiful person ever, and they put him on Death Row along with men who loved having someone this weak to play with.

I felt sorry for George when I read what his parents did to him as a child is all I can offer. I had no time to pity him as I had my own woes to think of. This man did the hardest time of all though, and many enjoyed making his life hell. I stayed out of it. George got stuck next to Roland in the second cell. They got along because Roland easily manipulated George to get things from him from the food trays we were served.

It was like 2 minutes after the guards left this time that I heard Roland already "working" George for whatever food items George was not allowed to eat, or did not care for when food would be served later. Roland offered George his fruits and George offered like 10 items in return. Life can be so petty and cheap, so things like Roland getting extras was a real important thing to this con man.

Roland knew he had just struck gold with this fool's bartering which he had just done. Like I said, they all preyed on George.

Once they put that 7th guy in the last empty cell on our pod, the guards went on to fill up the next pod across from ours on the unit.

Soon after they slid our pod doors shut on either side it was Dave who pointed out that the guy who was already in the one cell between he and Rump was occupied by Gary.

It began as Dave called it out to Rump, saying; 'Look who we got in our pod'!

I knew we had one leftover guy in there who was at Pittsburgh all along. I got back on my door to listen to Dave and Rump.

All of us except George were standing at our doors. Dave started calling to Gary and saying he should come to the door and talk to us about this place. What was the routine he asked. Gary blanked Dave and we all sort of chuckled at Dave for being blanked.

I am only telling you what Gary looked like for now. There was a reason they left him at Pittsburgh Penitentiary and there is a reason I am leaving why he got to death row out for a second or two from this story. You'll see why later.

I never met the infamous Gary before then, as I was in a different jail than he was. This was someone whom I knew nothing about personally. Since he was first there, Sergeant Rage spared him from a big introduction to any of us anyway.

Anyway, once all 48 cells were filled by men who were all like those I described here, they soon served us all food. Everything was a bustle for us then, as we got our personal belongings given back to us afterwards, while we also got our prison issued items given to us for our cells.

Then an hour or so they explained the new routine to us all.

1. Because of the limited space, 4 men would be put into a cage outside on the top of the roof for exercise 2 hours at a time. No more one man to one cage, (like how it was back at Huntingdon), this was going to be 4 men at a time in a ridiculously small cage. There were four cages outside. This was going to be madness!

2. If you did not want to be outside in the cages (taking your chances with three sick minded killers and no guard to watch over you in a cage), you could have 2 hours of "day-room" time. This was the enclosed area in front of each of the 3 pods located on the South side of the unit where I was housed. The other 3 pods had no metal tables or stools in them for day-room.

3. One phone was in the day-room on 3 pods within them. If you wanted to make a call, you had to negotiate it with the other 3 men who were put in the day-room with you for the 2 hours time allowed. It was up to you to be able to get your own share of time on the phone.

4. You were allowed to come out of your cell and go into the shower area 3 times per week. You would not be handcuffed while out of your cell, but if you leave the pod for exercise or any other reason, you were handcuffed in front.

5. You were allowed 2 hours per week of time in the "law library" with one other man. This was a set of secure rooms that had law books in it. This was where men helped one another with their legal problems and also they sometimes performed most of the sex acts on each other here.

6. Nothing left the unit. This meant that whatever happened on the top floor of this place stayed there. If you broke this last rule for any reason (and made these men risk losing the most easy job they ever had), you were to suffer like never before.

Now all of these 6 rules were shouted at us by the unit Sergeant. (Mr. Rage) as he came to be known to us all. He always had to shout things loudly. He always wore these big, thick soled boots on his feet to try and meet someone's chin level as well. Nasty mouthed bastard of a man with bright eyebrows and matching mustache that made him look like Captain Crunch was now a prison guard. He was about 140 pounds of constant trouble who stood about 5 foot 7.

Sgt. Rage loved this place. It was his playground to be frank about this point. Not a single inmate's letter went out that he did not read first, and not a phone call was made that he and his boys were not listening in on.

If you got a juicy letter from a lady friend, Sgt. Rage got on the intercom in your cell and read it to you while saying how hard his dick was from her words. If you wrote something about his unit to anyone outside, he read that to you as well, all while telling you how you were going to pay for your fuck up.

My best memory of him was of his reading my mother's letter to me one day soon after being there. Stupidly I pushed the button of my intercom and told him how he was making my dick hard along with his. Him and his favorite goon of a guard broke two of my lower teeth for that. I did not push the button many times after that incident.

The Unit had a lieutenant who showed up from time to time from his office located out in the Hallway. He was a wanna be "pretty boy" with a weight problem. He got bars on his shoulders for owning a college degree.

The Lieutenant was a white guy from the Pittsburgh area which was easy to know right off from his accent. He stood at about 5 foot 9 and was close to 250 pounds. This was a guy who's ass was in a chair all day. He had normal shoulders and legs, but his ass was huge! He also was dating a nurse in the jail right then, and he felt like he was all 'big man on campus' for this reason.

I learned one thing true while doing time in the joint, and that is that the higher you get in rank, the more someone else does your job. This guy was so lazy that he had everyone do his job for him.

At the age of 30 years old this guy that was our unit lieutenant was going to be a total blob of a human by the time his middle age hit. He even ate trays of food meant for prisoners on our unit by having the kitchen send up 52 meals for only 48 men on his block.

Basically Sgt. Rage ran this place along with 4 of his best drinking buddies after work while the Lieutenant signed off on it all. Sgt. Rage had it down then as his minions would jump to work with him on any prisoner with their clubs or fists. The one thing that was made to be understood over and over, was that no one told what happened on this floor beyond these men.

Now, I just came from a prison that was shut down after the United Nations had to even get involved by condemning it for it's "active practices of torture".

I was really disillusioned that right away, this place was clearly going to be worse than my previous situation!

I had just served 12 of the hardest years of my life on a prison unit called "B-block". That place had an average rate of survival of just 5 years for men housed there.

This was not making sense to me.

I was sitting on my bed wondering how this all came about when it became obvious.

My heart sank when I saw they had put us all into the hands of men that were prison guards who were themselves to be considered the "Worst of the Worst".

I will tell you now that I consider myself "lucky" that over the course of the next 3 years, how I got out of there with *only* 11 broken bones, a razor slash on my neck and face, while having 2 of my teeth broken. Lucky I tell you. That's damn right folks. I am one of the lucky ones able to get past this and tell all of you now what a nasty ordeal I found myself handling.

3. "LET THE LIONS LOOSE"!

Okay, so on my "little pod of murderers" that I lived on in 1995 we got Roland, George, then Keith to my left. Then my cell in the center, followed by Rump, a still silent Gary, and then finally Dave, with Bobby to finish off the guest list on my right. The set daily routine goes like this:

Each morning our routine began with a 6:30am wake up head count. On your feet and show some teeth.

At 7: am The Sergeant comes past and opens the pie holes on all 8 cells. As he is doing this, he is writing down who wishes to exercise outside in the cages, vs who wants to take their chances in the Day-room on a clipboard that he is holding in his hands. He also is collecting mail from the doors being sent out.

Right behind him then comes these aluminum carts that are about 6 feet high with steam coming off of them like a locomotive train. They are full with food trays on them. They come into the pod with a guard in front pulling each one. In comes the food with the guard holding a huge steel pitcher of Coffee in his free hand.

First gurad slides a tray in the cell pie-hole and moves two cells up. A second officer behind him pushing the same cart also has a huge pitcher of coffee in his free hand. He gets to put a tray every other cell that the first one passes so that they can keep it moving fast. They go past *one* time, you get what you get *one* time, because this train does not slow down. If you missed anything, or got a tray that has a missing item, shut the fuck up.

In goes the trays, and out comes your cup for your coffee, then slam! They closed the pie-hole. No stopping and your bitch ass fingers better grab that cup quick, or it too got slammed shut in the pie hole. They were that brutal. Meet "Frick and Frack". These 2 officers who were daily visitors to the unit. Both huge, both menacingly similar.

At 9:am after they had collected your trays, you got ready to be part of, or you were the witness to the next 2 hours of watching 4 men in front of your cells in the day-room. This was meant for their "exercise time" according to law, which said that they were to be given regularly. The law states that 22 hours in the cell, and 2 hours out 5 days a week was "fair".

All 4 men were meant to exercise in a 10 foot by 10 foot squared caged area outside. Pittsburgh had no room for this.

Instead, men were meant to enter an area with a big metal table centered there, with metal stools around it indoors. In other words, they all sat and played cards or they stood and talked to men locked in their cells on these 'day-room pods' during this period. The talking was done by shouting loudly over one another in as rude and as uncaring of a manner as one could contrive.

It was the day-room where most of the murders would happen in this building. The "outside exercise cages" which were filled up outside with up to 16 men divided up into the 4 cages were actually safer than the day-room.

In the day-room men could slide your enemy a knife or other small weapons that could fit through the heavy wire of the cage that it was all made of. Then you got all stabbed up while the guy who gave your enemy the blade laughs it up.

In the day-room you can also get boiling hot oil or other things thrown in your eyes by the inmate who is out for his shower while you are stuck in the day-room cage.

You may get stomped to death in the outdoor cages by 3 other men if they all turn on you at once, but at least that was the lesser of your chances to be killed here.

Oh, and you can also be raped in the cages by two men, while the third companion of theirs keeps checking for the guards to come break it up outside. I had to witness this once when a guy named William got raped by two guys in the cages with him, and that was just days after we got there as well.

Now, if you do not come out of your cell, you do not get a phone call. If you want that phone call, you gotta come out and "play" in the day-room. I don't know about how the others felt, but the idea of me talking to my mother or someone whom I loved on a phone felt ugly right then. Especially while 3 predators circled around me, all waiting for their share of time on the phone or a chance to kill me.

Don't slip up and turn your head around towards the mesh wire or lean down at the base of the phone to try to hear clearly. What I mean is, do not try to speak quietly to your party on the phone with your back to anyone. If you do that simple stupid move, and someone sees the back of your neck sticking out... you are done. You NEVER turn your back on anyone while inside day-room, ever. Not once.

Most days by 1: pm in the afternoon, all the drama of inmate movement is over and they shut the whole place down by 3: pm. That is it. Just a skeleton crew on after that 3: pm time and no one moves on the floor.

They turn out the day-room lights by 5:pm and you are all down for the night.

That is when you noticed the constant noise of the vents the most. See, once all 48 cells were filled up with prisoners, each one the men did like me, and blocked up the 18 inch by 28 inch air vent blowing right down on your bed. If you were the only guy who did not block your vent, you had 30 mph air blowing on you all day. In summer it was cold air, so you froze your ass off if your vent had no cover. In winter time you baked and had nose bleeds and headaches and your skin turned ashy from being dried out constantly.

In order to block your vent in your cell you made "squares" of toilet paper about 3 inches in diameter. You soaked them in your sink until they could be molded. You then mashed them against the metal mesh wire inside the vent opening, forcing the paper into whatever crevices there were in the metal until it stuck into it. It takes one and a half rolls of toilet paper to cover your vent. You had 36 squares to make a cover for.

Still the noise from the giant air ducts roared all day...

The only time when this noise all came to a halt was actually what kicked everything off on our pod really. It lead to the first death of one of my 7 companions, and this was just four months after I got there.

When you had no TV or radio for breaking the rules, (or some guard just wanted you to go 60 days without these things for their own time to torment you)...you were at the mercy of the other 7 men on your pod. They could could make sure that you had to hear them all day long, while you had nothing to cut if off from this "mind fuck" effort, unless of course you want to flush your toilet 400 times in a row.

Gary was the first one who endured this painful point from us 7 fellow men on our pod. It happened when he had nothing in his cell except sheets and a towel. It was then that we others feasted on him in an orgy of sarcasm. In my first month there Gary was taking "too long" going to the shower one day, as he stopped to talk to another inmate. It was George whom he was all chatty with. He was trying to talk to George about not talking to the blacks prisoners on the pod, as Gary was working on George with his racist bullshit. Gary's doing so within our unit that day was enough for the guard on duty to not like it, so the guard put him on disciplinary time for "refusing to obey a direct order".

Oh how we all loved to get digs in on Gary then, and we sure delighted in making him feel low for the things he did to end up on Death Row. He had to sit in an empty cell listening to us all talking about his crimes and laugh about him for hours.

We all knew his story and nobody liked Gary. Fuck Gary we all thought. He had 60 good days of us telling his story to each other, all while mocking his loony mind.

Yeah well, we taught Gary something when we did that to him:

He knew from being there before we got there, that when we all had no radio or TV, how he was going to get back at us. The way in which we had tormented him was nothing compared to how he could get us all back at once for what we did to him.

You see, the prison was so old and what with it being located on the banks of the huge Ohio river...Rivers flood, don't they? Gary knew this from being there before us. In Pittsburgh, the city is built on the confluence of 3 rivers actually. So basically, yes every winter, we had some power cuts due to flooding that we had to deal with inside the jail.

I wasn't really keen to learn all of this my first year there.

It was only until the next time that the power went out did I sincerely regret fucking with my man Gary. He taught me a lesson about delighting in others suffering with schadenfreude joy. He made me hope for him to rot in hell, with him all twisted in agony for it too, you nutty bastard...

The day it all happened, and how you finally *now* get to learn about our companion Gary as well as his back story, is like this:

Everything went dead. Lights, noise, everything. Then the security lights popped on and we were all bathed in yellowish light.

I thought to myself: 'Oh shit, wonder how long we gotta go without power and what the hell had caused it all to cut off'? That was back when it had all clicked silent initially, about 6:am one morning. My ears were instantly ringing just then, like I had just came out of a rock concert. You can actually hear silence in that moment. I got up off of my bed and I looked out of my cell door to the control unit through glass panels of the hallway.

Only emergency lighting was on, so in the dim yellow of what I could see, the officer was walking "180" as we called it. He was scanning back and forth to keep check on the 3 of the 6 pods that were on this side of the unit.

He was able to see, but he could not now activate the intercom to hear anything inside of the pods. I tugged on my door to see if it had popped open from the release of the electrics. Nope. Nothing.

Everything was so still and quiet that no one spoke for quite a while. We all were so aware that we lived in such an abnormal setting that we were stunted when the constant noise ceased to drive it all. We were waiting to see if the power would come back on for so long that we all stayed in a quiet waiting game.

That was when Gary came to his door and began to torment all 7 of us. Here finally is his background and why it was so important to tell it all to you now. It is the basis of why so much made me sick to my stomach to recall.

What Gary did to other humans was not done for the usual motives that others go to prison for doing.

It was not for sexual needs or "power over others" in some mere act of dominance. That was too common for the likes of this madman. He had a plan that was insane, one given to him by God almighty no less.

Here is how it all unfolded...

Gary went to prison in 1979. While inside of jail then, he did stock trades from his cell and he made good money off of the silver and gold futures markets. He was getting disability payments monthly from the US military as well, after he was diagnosed and having schizophrenia. He used this money while in prison to invest in stocks. By the time Gary left Graterford prison in 1983, he had nearly half a million dollars.

Now, from guys who knew of him then whom I did time with, they all said he got done wrong many times over by black prisoners while inside. You see, Gary was in jail for the wrongest crime there was to be incarcerated for when it comes to be locked up inside prisons that were dominated by black inmates. Gary had a bad time in jail because he made a huge mistake in who he had victimized *outside* being black.

Why? Because in 1978 Gary went to a mental institution located in New Jersey and signed his black girlfriend's mentally impaired sister out of the hospital. Gary then put the poor woman in a cage in his basement and he sexually abused her while holding her captive for endless hours of fun with his victim.

When she was finally rescued by authorities and returned to the hospital, they found out then that she had not only been sexually abused, but that she was pregnant with Gary's child as well.

Gary was given 3 to 7 years sentence for the crimes of unlawful imprisonment and sexual assault. He even paid a fellow inmate to help him get his time cut on appeal, so when the crack epidemic hit America in 1982, (where the prisons went from 1 million prisoners, to 2 million prisoners seemingly overnight), Gary got out early in 1983 with all that money from his stock trades.

Gary was going to get revenge on every black dude who had raped him in jail. Gary was going to get everybody who ever did him wrong in life back as well. You see, this man truly was insane. No one understood what he was about to do once set free from that first jail sentence.

Moving right into the heart of a black neighborhood in North Philadelphia, Gary set up his new place of torture and sexual amusement. He even bought a broken down Rolls Royce car from the police impound yard auctions. He had a Cadillac engine fitted into it to make it run again. And just like the car, everything was for a reason, as it was all part of his plan to start hunting.

Gary was in his 40's and was cleaned up enough back then to use his appearance (and the car) to start picking up black prostitutes. Tall and dark hair he was over 6 feet tall.

Gary groomed the women whom he wanted to keep, and soon made sure that they would not be sought heavily if they were to go missing. He learned all of this from his doing research on their backgrounds, should they be the ones which he wanted. He even purchased a mail-order bride from the Philippines whom he married and began pimping on the streets of Philly. After cocaine made his already crazy mind worse, Gary went berserk and beat his new wife nearly to death. She and her unborn son soon fled the house and police nearly found his "Den of hell" under the house right then.

That was when he lost it. Gary went "next level". He soon decided to finally come out of his shell and teach us all whom he really thought that he was. He started collecting his slaves one by one, until he had 5 of them held hostage in his basement under his house. He dug a huge pit several feet deep in the basement so they could not climb out.

The women whom Gary had abducted all had to be able to produce children for him. This was very important to him now that he had lost his new half-cast child when his mail order bride fled. When this was shown to not be possible with any of the women whom he had abducted, he went berserk on them.

Gary electrocuted one victim to death whom had lied to him about her ability to give him children in front of the others. He also strangled another woman to death for this same reason in front of the others as well.

All of the surviving women were then put on a diet of dog food which was mixed up with the human remains of his victims whom he had killed. All of which were prepared by Gary in his kitchen. He then went on to abuse them for months while trying to breed them in this filthy pit which they were made to live in. I could only image how these poor women endured what he did to them. I lived 3 cells away from this guy and I could see him every time I stood at my door if he was at his door at the same time while we were getting our food trays. I walked past him daily.

I shared the same re-filtered air as Gary did when we stood next to one another during those times our cells were searched weekly.

We looked at one another, but no talking ever. I made him know not to try that racist shit on me, so he knew better than to speak to me from my looks aimed at him. I was glad that I was in on that first incident of messing with him early on, when he had no TV or radio, as it spared me having to interact with him on a familiar level afterwards I felt.

I did not enjoy my feelings which I had for long after that day when we lost power though. And much to my horror I was to discover, (you can look it up in the press as it was big news that particular year), all 3 rivers overflowed their banks that winter, and the entire sub basement of Pittsburgh Penitentiary was submerged in water.

The power generator of our building being underground meant that it too was submerged under water. The flood waters took days to even receded, so our power in the building was cut off and we went without energy for 9 days in total.

Gary did not have a few hours to get back at us, this shit was about to go on day and night for*ever* man.

It got so sickening at some points, that men were making themselves hoarse with efforts of scream at him for what he was saying.

This next bit is additionally what was setting us all off in torment for how he went on and on in a performance...

Gary put on a "performance" of a lifetime alright. He took center stage and he let rip on us for over a week.

He would start with the mocking tone he used to mimic the terrified voices of his victims lying in chains while inside of his basement torture chamber. He painted the picture of them conversing about him, along with his adding how he knew what they were saying all along, as he laid for hours on the floor above listening through a hole which he had cut there for this reason.

This first voice he used was deep and powerful. I can still recall every detail when I try hardest not to, but as best I can never forget, here is how he did it: 'God gave me my slaves'!

(Gary switching into falsetto impersonation of the first victim soon after)

'Oh Girl, this man crazy, he gonna kill us all, how we gonna get out of here'...

(Then Gary in an slightly deeper falsetto voice of a second woman answering the first)

'Shhh, please don't let him hear us talking honey, I am just praying to God he is gonna stop'!

Then that was when Gary did the "overview voice" of his own natural one for us again, where he had to take that tormentors image he had just painted in those victim's voices, and then drive it in deeper by going back to being the narrator of this sick tale.

He did so with mocking laughter of how he was going to kill them. He did it hoping that we then all had to imagine what he was doing to these black women in torment. He then drove it into us further with how he laughingly played out his sick ritual on them because they were his "Black Piggy's".

He would begin always with his snide laugh that was purely put on before saying over and over:

'I own you bitches by *right',* and then, 'I am going to teach you why God chose me above all men to breed you'! (By this point he knew to wait for whatever screamed obscenities were dying down before he went on..'I am your MASTER, you filthy Niggers'! 'God put me here to use you to create the MASTER race'!

Gary then explained how the "mud" people needed to be bred off the earth with a superior seed. He told the victims that their only hope was to be made pure by having him and other white men breed a master race.

I kicked the cell door along with others at first, I flushed my toilet like they did too, and I drove my fingers into my ears to try and blot out his voice as I bet most of the others did as well. None of it worked.

Why?

Because imagine what it was like when the guards even helped Gary out by pulling out the ones who were kicking hard on their cell doors to give them a beat down while Gary laughed over it?

Oh they let Gary keep right on with his crap and he said shit over and over without them saying a word to him. Why? Because they saw what he was doing and they loved it. Gary was doing ten times the work which they could do to us in one day of his torment, than it would take them a year to do to us.

So, kick too hard on your cell door and YOU get your ass whipped before being tossed back into your cell to the delight of Gary laughing. Or like me, you just gritted your teeth and you took it as best you could.

Gary had it down then. He had a set way to tell us what he did, but more importantly to him, we were going to be exclusively privileged to know his plan in detail. Each time he did his "routine" It took about 15 good minutes where he added all his most important bits.

By the 3rd day of this unending performance, many had just given up trying to drown him out. That never made Gary any less determined to drive it into our brains over and over.

If the nurse came by with the Lieutenant he stopped long enough to take his medications and then Gary went right back at it. I know it shouldn't be funny to think this shit then. but man crazy people can go on physically for hours and hours on end, whereas a normal person would wear down!

I mean, I can kick off in anger. But 20 minutes later, I am "done with all that shit" and I just say 'whatever' then and go about my business...but crazy people like Gary have some sort of "Monster-Energy-Drink" thing going on in their blood. It's where they can go for days with the same insane repeated acts or words, all while drunk on the power of some shit that we know *nothing* about!

I was wondering if at some point if Gary was even worried that they would finally put the lights and power back on, as he sure seemed rushed at times to get his act of his all down without a misquoted word.

Gary seemed to think that his favorite part of his over all performance was his describing for us how he had "juiced the bitch".

This was his way to describe for us how he wrapped an electrical chord around a woman's throat and he plugged it in to the wall socket to kill her. He delighted in saying how he had killed her in a puddle of the...(May God help me for sharing this)...in a puddle of the urine that was inside the bottom of the pit which these other poor women were chained to the bottom of.

Gary made any black dude on that unit want to kill him for how he said this poor lady gurgled and flopped around on the floor like a big fat fish. I wished I had a chance to have gotten to him right then for how angry it made me just hearing him laugh over it. I felt really bad for my fellow prisoners who were born of black mothers who had to hear this crap over the years before me.

I know it was bad for how I nearly cried in frustration by the end of it all. This went on to be the sickest time of my life. I never before truly went into much detail over this event out of all of the many prison stories that I have shared. It was always just so sick to recall, that for years I tried to pull back from letting it out I guess.

I stood at my door at one point during that week to take time out to watch Gary perform his act without letting it affect me as best that I could while observing his actions.

Gary really struggled to make sure that he had his details correct in his way of doing this act under such a strident level. So much so, that he was telling this whole thing like it was his most fervent belief system which he could keep hold of inside of his mind.

I watched intently as he described grinding up a human being into food, I saw the sinister way in how he made a joke of chopping her up. I have to admit, I felt so much pity for the women, that I tried to imagine what it was like to be held truly captive by this guy as I stood there before him.

I found myself transfixed there in a detached way by doing this observation technique. It was a time where I could look at this man before me and just picture him as he once was, back in his basement while frothing mad with anger. I could really picture him unleashing all of this fury on his victims then. The fact that in his mind that somehow, God himself had given Gary a mandate to create a new race by doing all of this sick shit, all just made it extra creepy to me to imagine as he spoke about his reasons.

At one point, I did notice that Gary really reacted to anyone mentioning his child, or how they were going to get his child in revenge if they ever got out of jail. He revved his rhetoric up then, he really reacted with venom to that sore spot I noticed.

He had a favorite target most days, that of the only black inmate we had on the pod being Roland. Always in retort to this, it was Roland who was the one who kept asking Gary how his child was doing. I was not at first sure which child Roland was referring to, then Roland shouted about the handicapped woman Gary had raped and this really set Gary off. Roland said he could not even have a male child and only had to baby whores for other men to breed. Then of course Roland asked where was this superior generation of supremacist kids that Gary had made? Why did they let their messiah suffer?

I think Gary hated both his inability to have made any male children from his captives this last time, as well as how the two he had sired (with his Philippine wife as well as his ex girlfriend's abducted sister) were also taken from him before he could poison their minds. When you see how this all comes back on Gary later, it won't matter what he said to Roland as a comeback.

When the power finally returned on the unit Sergeant Rage knew we were all going to get Gary back for this shit. They moved him on the other side of the unit, well away from us all.

Everything was different for us somehow, even though they moved him away. What we all had just gone through day after day, of listening to a man describe with glee all the horrors you never want stuck in you head, we were all emotionally or mentally violated it seemed.

I did not hear anyone have much to say for days in the aftermath of Gary obliterating our heads with his sickness. I guess that was his parting present to us all for thinking that we had the upper hand over him.

That was the quiet time, right before all sorts of sick attacks on each other on the unit jumped off. It was like we could not take it out on the bastard who wound us all up, so we then turned on each other instead.

Because just as soon as they started up our routines again, all manner of mayhem erupted. It was like Gary had ripped the lid off of a hornets nest. Soon we were all going to act like the sickest bastards ever, now that we had been used and toyed with by the staff with Gary's shit.

Poor George was the first one to find out how all of the rules were now completely off of the table. He went into the day-room soon after the power outage incident was over.

George went there to try to use the phone to tell his family that he was okay. Bobby got angry at him without much provoking when he said how George wasn't touching the phone before he had a chance to use it. George tested him and tried to use the phone anyway since he had already gotten through to his family...

Bobby had calmly let George get all the way through to his party on the phone, then stealthily walked over to where he was behind George in his wheel chair.

First Bobby took off his prison Jumpsuit, along with his giant T-shirt and stripped down to boxers shorts only. His huge hairy chest and belly were a shock against his super white skin.

Bobby then tossed his sweat stained T-Shirt over George's head, as he then punched George about 6 or 7 times in the back of his head to knock him out. It was sick to see a man in a wheelchair being abused like this. Bobby began force-ably orally sodomizing George in the day-room right there in front of our cells. Roland was in the day-room with them and thought that it was so funny to watch, that when Bobby finished, Roland took his turn abusing George.

Then, after Roland had a turn on George's face, Bobby then wheeled the poor man over to where the phone was still dangling, and he beat George in the head with the phone while shouting "HelllllllO"!!!, to anybody still on the line on not during this sick moment.

When Keith saw that shit going down with a fellow crippled inmate being abused right in front of his own cell, I knew he was thinking that he was next. I knew that he saw also, how the guards in the control booth right at that very minute of the assault were also mimicking how Bobby had just face-fucked George. The guards were mocking it all in a parody which they were doing on each other while inside of the control booth. When Keith said to me 'This is too sick to be real' in a pitiful voice, I knew that he felt that there was no hope for him now.

I was going to get Bobby some payback for that shit that he had just done to George. I was already going to do Roland wrong any chance that I had, just out of self preservation, but I saw somebody had to stop Bobby before he went way too far. If not, it was only going to be a matter of time until he went through all of the others, only to then find time to "play" with me.

Look, I have to tell you the outcome of Gary's fate a bit later on so that we can see how he lined up in this little mad procession to be the second man killed in Pennsylvania.

But for now, because of what happened to George as soon as we had gotten power again, I gotta now stick to Keith's story. I have to explain how he was the first guy to die, and how it was all because of that sexual assault on George.

I would not have been hurt had it been Gary going first to his death, but that was just me wanting to get him out of my head... No, that very first guy to die was going to be Keith in just a few months of us being here. And while his was the first death of the men with whom I was housed along with while inside of Pittsburgh Penitentiary, his is also the one that I still struggle with the most some nights...

3. KEITH TOOK *HIS* WAY OUT

Keith was not built for this shit. This guy was not a monster and nor was he a madman either. He was just one single stupid act in his life away from being you or I folks.

In prison there are 4 ways that you can escape being there for the average person such as Keith was.

First, you go on living with a complex belief system that you will get out. A real phenomenon is when you ask a guy on Death Row what his chances are of survival, and they had a set way of telling you that if "this and that happen", (or if the appeals courts only focus on what they say is the *real* points), how they are going home. Not getting just a lesser sentence mind you, they will tell you how they are going **home** period.

Then there is the people who come up with "The Blur" as I call it. Using things like endless hours of watching TV or playing chess with another guy are common. Men will do all manner of things to make themselves not think about how they are getting their life crushed daily.

I know of men who watched TV for up to 18 hours a day, and if they had no TV, they quickly went mentally dark afterwards. It was like that TV box was the only reality that they wanted to know of.

If none of that works, you take handfuls of pills given to you free by the staff. The little blue ones make you sleep for up to 12 hours a day, as the rest of your time is a fog inside of your brain. I saw men check out on the "Little Blue Express" as we called it, for years and years. Once you go down the pills route, you never come back to anything close to normal.

Last then comes religiosity.

Oh the fervent way in which men will all of a sudden grasp fiendishly to God, or any kind of way to escape their fate with a new religious convictions. It does not matter how many people you butchered to get your criminal convictions. All you have to do is you say some words to an imagined "being" in the sky, and you have all your blood stained deeds wiped away!

These men can pop on some new head garment to pray with after giving their parents birth name "a heave-ho" and they get to sit next to their victims in the afterlife then, all as a reward from your new identity. Just like that, some magic words spoken here on Earth, and WHAM!,you are forgiven now.

These men actually believe you and your murdered victims are as equal in love once again in God's eyes from their now adopting prayer. Because of the guilty survivor, you all get to sit on a big bench in harmony somewhere in Heaven forever and ever, amen.

I have seen some world class actors playing the "religiosity game" while in a cell. I have witnessed men trying valiantly to become pious for understanding God in their efforts to pay for what they did beside them. I believe God is proven in E=Mc Squared.

Either way, this is still the last of the mentally driven escapes from prison that you can come up with. I personally believe in my spirituality without any claim of being better than another person for it. All I ever prayed for was "Good".

I honestly believe it was having no way to "blur" reality (that truly could help him escape from this place) which made Keith want to die right away. When Gary tortured us all for so long, followed by Bobby then showing us all how the guards were in on this sick joke of an experiment was too much for him. I think Keith figured that this zoo was beyond his ability to cope. He had no way to defend himself with 3 other psychos in the cages or in the day-room with him being helpless to stop anything.

Keith had no chance to live in a place where just going to the shower was not only agony with his hip being shattered, but it was a good place for him to get hurt seriously by another inmate. Keith turned to me for answers for weeks in our vents after that assault on George.

I was dealing with some pretty bleak shit right then myself though, as one guards on the block had it in for me it seemed. I did not know what had started it off, but this guy was making my life hell right away. So when Keith started telling me how he knew that he could no longer take it, I offered to get him some weed from population sent over, or some tranquilizer pills from George (or one of the others) who took them.

I told Keith that he should just take a bunch of his own pain pills. along with a bunch of other pills that we could barter for, and just go quietly in his sleep.

I even said that I would make him some jailhouse "hooch" from grapefruit sections and bread mixed with sugar, all sealed in plastic bags for him to have a drink of booze if he wished. I said we could have a nice party for him and he could just check out of this hotel in a nice sleepy way.

Keith said that as a Christian, that he was not able to kill himself no matter what his ordeal. That he had to obey God's law. I told him that I would have a think about it. I told him I couldn't just strangle him, nor was I going to knife his ass if he wanted me to. He laughed of course, knowing then that I was cracking silly jokes.

But then he said...(as I had heard him say many times)...'Oh man, *why* did I do it'?!

I knew then to leave Keith be, as that was what he always said in retrospect to himself when he thought about why he had been so stupid as to kill his only childhood friend.

One night, after one of the many conversations that we had together (which was almost always done through the vents as we each lay in bed at night) in that spring of 1995, I crawled back over to Keith at the vent once. I sat close up to where I could see where he lay on his mattress before I spoke.

I had nearly stopped for the night, but the way he was so down mentally just drew me over to his side of my cell. I said: "I think you should hear something I planned".

I could see his chest and lower body through my vent clearly as Keith was laying half propped up on his pillow on his bunk. I knew he was in a lot of pain as he had to lay on his side constantly. He was getting bed sores from the side of his body that was not the one with the fractured bones which he could actually lay on.

I told Keith that I too had read the bible several times by that point. I told him that maybe I could help him in his search for answers for what I had planned.

Keith and I then talked for hours that night. I took breaks to make coffee at times, and I sat there going over and over it with him. I even got out the Bible and read to him a part which I knew had to make sense to him about my point.

I did all that I could to really work on him, and at the same time, try to make him strong in the ways in which he told me that he needed to be for accepting what I had to offer.

It was nearly morning when, in a croaking and very tired voice, Keith said that he was starting to try and get on his feet for head count. I left him to his wobbling efforts to do so, as I then went and sat on my bed. I was so worn thin by what I just went through in talking to this man, that I stood up and just began to mindlessly walk back and fourth for hours.

Even though I was exhausted, I did my routine. Take 5 paces one way, a turn on your heel, and then 4 paces back. Anyone says they do five one way, and five back the other way is lying. It's just how it is.

All morning long I kept walking. I knew that each hour of steps was about 1 half mile of taking five paces by four paces. I wanted to sleep all that day so I kept at it until after day-room was done. Once they started shutting the unit down in the evening I slowed down and then stopped when they turned off the lights. I stripped out of my sweat soaked clothes. I then bathed in my sink and went to bed. I heard not one peep from Keith that day, nor many more in the next few weeks after that night.

Of all the people to be an asshole about this next bit soon afterwards, it was the Lieutenant who came on the pod instead of Sgt. Rage to open all the pie-holes one morning. That was rare.

When he got to Keith's door he shouted 'Good morning you DEAD Motherfucker'!

He then followed it on with 'Oh *FINALLY*'! And then lastly he said; 'I love this asshole', 'he's the *one*'!

I knew before he had finished what he was yelling about.

I knew before Dave asked the Lieutenant what was going on, exactly what he was going to come out of his fat-assed mouth with in reply to Dave's question. I did not have to wonder, I just *knew* what was coming.

The Lieutenant announced to us 8 men at once that his morning was made ever so much brighter by the mornings news broadcast. Keith had just had his Death Warrant signed by the Governor the news said. The best part for the Lieutenant was how Keith was going to be put to death later that same month of May 1995! I was sick to my stomach that it was *that* fast.

I mean, we had just gotten to the unit a few months prior and they had just changed the method of execution from being electrocuted to death, to now having lethal injection. All of the court battles were not even over as to be even certain if the State were even allowed to do this new method of killing prisoners. Then all of a sudden, thanks to Keith, here they are now getting the green light to carry out all of the executions in this new way.

Everyone kept quiet, as no one liked a member of staff being all pumped up at one of our deaths. We all fought like a bucket of crabs among each other but when the staff singled one out like this, we all knew we could be that "one guy", so we hardly let it make us join them.

I knew in my heart that Keith was as embarrassed as hell to not only have us all learn about this in how it came out that morning. Soon everyone was going to learn that all this shit was Keith volunteering to go to his death was affecting their appeals.

Keith decided to be the first man executed in Pennsylvania in 25 years rather than live like this on my pod. That is what drove him. Keith also knew how every man on that unit was going to feel like he had just made it possible for all of them to be lined up and killed next. He broke the stalemate that had been going on for years with the State unable to kill a prisoner. He broke the code and he gave up first. He was a coward who had let every murderer feel closer to their own end in this way. They all felt this about Keith. He had zero friends right then it looked to all.

I sat on my bunk and did not try to speak to Keith in the vent after that incident. He did not answer any of the men who paraded past his door that day who were shouting at him for being a pussy. Nor did Keith respond to the ones begging him to stop "giving the man what he wants". When a prisoner like Keith has nothing to say to anything that anyone says to him, I learned that it means that the man has his mind already made up.

So then it all came oh so fast.

It was a blink in time that the day came, with guards pouring into the pod real early in the morning to take Keith out of Pittsburgh. His was set for transfer to his final destination to be taken out to Rockview prison. That place was in the center of the state and is isolated as hell. That is where the old electric chair was located and that was where they had a nice new way to stick poison in your veins. Either way was meant to cut off your life in that"Death Chamber" located within that prison.

It was just like somehow this had all been just the other day or so before, when Keith talked to me through the vents in our cells. When all the guys tried to talk to Keith about his decision to die early on, we thought this would drag out for months. There were dudes who came around after the first day that they found out about his decision. They were ready to act. One even begged him to come to the yard so they could snuff him out, if he "just needed to die".

I swear to God, the way they offered to do his murder was like they were doing him a favor by "hooking him up". Doing him this big *favor*!? Man, that's cold.

Look, there was this guy who was really afraid to be executed named Frank .

Frank was this 5 foot 9 white guy who weighed no more than 150 lbs. He was convicted of repeatedly slashing a gay man's throat with a box cutter some years back, in an area just outside of Philadelphia. He was standing in the day-room outside of Keith's cell one day when he says to Keith (who is laying in his cell with his cell light out, as if he wants no one to talk to him)....

'Keith, I know you can hear me...listen', (pause) 'I know you don't know me, but I have to tell you something'... (no need for Frank to get a reply, as he had what he was gonna say all rehearsed), he plowed right on...

'Yeah, so listen Keith, come to the Law Library tomorrow', 'I can slit your throat with a razor blade'. 'I can even put your head over the waste bucket in the library so that the blood will be all inside of it'... a brief pause again...Nothing from Keith. Then, in the point to win the bid for his deed to be accepted Frank added: 'You don't have to look at it or *nothing*', 'it will be over quick'!

Keith never replied to any of this shit so Frank seemed let down that his efforts to save us all from the hang man fell short like this.

The others who laid down their offers to Keith were somewhat more blunt.

There was a guy named "Busthead" who said he was gonna kill Keith for wanting to die.

This guy had been put on Death Row for killing inmates in the past and I don't even know his real name...This guy loved his jailhouse name of "Busthead" though, as he loved to do just that. He busted people's heads.

At about 5 foot 10 and weighing 230 pounds, he was a round brown bi-product of crackhead mother mixed with heroin addicted father. Basically Busthead was a giant ball of anger from a nasty childhood that was spent in foster care.

Busthead shouted at Keith from the day-room one day in a different tactic. Busthead said that if he failed to get to Keith and murder him before the "police got him out of there", how he was gonna butcher Keith's mom if he got out of jail one day.

Then, when that failed to get a response from Keith, Busthead said he would have one of his boys who were outside right now go over to Keith's house where his parents lived next week. Told Keith how he would have his boys kill them all right now.

Here is how Mr. Busthead eloquently put it to Keith in a machine gun fast statement, all while standing in front of Keith's cell doing jumping jacks for his exercise:

After loudly bursting into the day-room shouting for "this white motherfucker" to wake up, and ignoring anyone else in the area , this maniac began with:

'Hey White Motherfucking, cracker-ass Devil, get your motherfucking honky ass up on your door, *now*!'

(That was half a notch higher than Busthead being his usual calm self when he was wanting to see someone at their door).

Today he was really full throttle screaming with anger driving him onwards.

When he found out that this white devil named Keith was putting him closer to his own "real death" (as Busthead described it), no fuckin' way was *he* letting this white cracker boy put him closer to *his* doom!

So there was Busthead, standing in the day-room demanding that Keith get his ass up so that he could explain to him how, if he went through with his white devil plan to "bring us *all* closer to dying", how Keith better expect his mom and dad to die as well.

Keith never answered and I kept my mouth shut along with all of the others on our pod during all of this time. Busthead had already killed other inmates for less than this, so a stabbing without it being a homicide for him was considered a slow week.

You knew this was one crazy bastard just to look at him before you, with his offset eyes, manic motions, set phrases of violence, all making him agitated looking. He had this look that was completed with a shaven head and the "no regard for human life" look that he proudly wore on his face.

Trust me, this guy was something else. Oh, and by the way, he was "forcefully gay" without care if you were as well, is all I am throwing out there. His favorite thing to do in prison was to grab a smaller man from behind, punch him in the back of the head until he is out cold. Then Busthead would bend him over while pulling his clothes off, and then orally eating his ass in front of others and raping him.

Anyway, Keith knew that he was going to go through with his sentence being carried out. He was going to be executed, so no threats by anyone there was going to make him fearful.

If it was me that was in Keith's shoes, I would have indulged.

Oh hell yes! If you know you are out of there, like my boy Keith knew that he was out of there, take some shots I say!

I would have told Busthead to try and brush his big nasty teeth after he had just finished force-ably eating another man's ass. I would have definitely told Frank to go and slit his own fuckin' throat, and what a sick fuck that he was for even asking to do that for me. But hey, that's just me I guess...

It went on like that for a while with Busthead, coming around for a few days taunting Keith. It never got beyond words though.

No one was able to stop Keith from being put to death, no matter the ploy or threats. I went on a mission mentally to stay well clear of it all with the other men when they tried to get me to talk him out of it. I did everything that I could to blot it all out in fact. I stopped talking to Keith for days and left him to it. I felt like there was nothing else that I could do at that point anyway.

On the morning that they came and moved Keith out of the cell on the pod, not one person spoke during the whole thing. Even the dickhead of a lieutenant from our pod was quieted as they had all of these officials on the unit making sure this was all captured on camera.

A procession of 6 Officers, 2 Sergeant's, as well as 2 lieutenants this time came, as well as the deputy Warden being there too.

They came with one of the officers holding a shoulder mounted cam-corder behind them all in a long procession. All of the men were very quieted on the unit as it was the Deputy Warden who told Keith that it was "time". The only words spoken were by this man the whole time. That was it. He said the words: "Keith"? Then: "It's *time*".

He waived his arm in the air to signal to the control booth, and Keith's door popped open. They went in to get him and it was so hushed afterwards as they emerged with him in chains then.

My balls shriveled up in my nut sack at that moment. I stood at my door with my fingers gripping the mesh in the slots as my forehead rested on the cool metal door. I was going to stand like that until Keith came by, but I kept going over and sitting on my bunk momentarily only to pop right back up and stand at the door again. It was really nerve wracking for me to get to see him one last time.

The guards had obviously went into Keith's cell and helped him up off the bed where he always lay with a bit of care it seemed. They came out of Keith's cell with an officer on either side, (holding an arm on each side) and him wearing handcuffs meekly in front of his body.

Keith had his eyeglasses askew on his face from getting up, so he kind of ducked his head to the left to even them up as he passed my cell. I got knots in my stomach watching his last footsteps in life. I made eye contact with him there and then. Just as I was about to say *whatever* it was that never came out of my mouth, Keith beat me to the punch.

Of all the things that I expected him to say to me, it was not what I had expected from him right then. I got a very sweetly stated line of: "Thanks Nick". That was all that I got from him.

I nearly shit my pants and my face lost all the blood in it as I went over and sat the fuck down. I fled as fast as my wobbly legs could manage from his words. That shit blasted my ears and made me run. I did not even say goodbye or anything when he hit me with that line.

Looking into a man's face as he walks to his death freaks you out, as it's like they touched some secret "thing" that you never want to hold. They are going where you are fighting to never go, and it creeps you to your core to know you have to go as well. Their willingness to go to this place makes you feel shamed and scared for feeling like you know it is coming your way soon, yet you never want to admit this.

I felt this awful chill pass by me when Keith and the execution team went by my cell door. I don't think that chill which I felt had anything to do with temperature. I swear that it felt like a huge ball of dead, or whatever "dead" is, had just rolled menacingly past me. I was afraid of it whether it was real or not.

At the door of the pod as they all left with Keith, I heard the officer say "MT" to the control booth officer. That was the 2 letters that they put on top of your cell door. That replaces where your name was written on the cell door in blue colored name-cards. All of our names were laid out on a board taped to the control panel located inside the booth. Keith was now gone so it was "MT" on that spot.

We got no exercise for a couple days following Keith being taken out to be executed. They wanted to give us all time to process his death, so they even had the unit psychologist come around to speak to us all if need be. I gave that a pass.

. The Lieutenant thought it was "cool" to have the front page of the news paper with Keith's execution on it's cover to be mounted and framed. He then placed it in his office so that each time we were taken out of the pod to the main hallway, we all saw it hanging there.

I should have known that newspaperon the wall inside the Lieutenant's office was a bad omen.

His doing that shitty thing, propelled every negative along further with the way the guards now were acting like this shit was "real" with executions being carried out. It was making all these guards act like since it was all so real, well then 'lets get it *on with doing more crazy acts on these motherfuckers*'!

They held us all in our cells for a few days after the incident, hoping to calm us all down. Yet that next week when they resumed our "routines" on that unit after Keith was executed, all hell broke loose. In one week alone, we had five straight days of serious violence kick off.

This was also the week that I made the most bitter enemy of a guard there. I did not do a single thing to provoke it happening either. I did not need to, as I had that cocksucker Roland on the pod doing his scheming on me. He now wanted to carry out *his* plans to finally see if he could murder me.

4. 'The worst place to shut your eyes'

How the hell that I managed to get through this next bit still makes me a bit proud of myself on one hand, while at the same time still wanting to shake my head in shame...

It was half way through the first day-room period on a Monday morning after Keith was executed that I heard the sounds of a fight kicking off in the pod next to ours. All the running foot steps sounds and keys jangling combined with the very distinct sound of metal clubs on flesh, (with those "thumps" that are low down on the sound range), all make this all a very familiar sound to know in jail.

I looked out my door and I saw two bloody messed up guys being pulled apart. I couldn't tell who was fighting with whom, but soon word spread from vent to vent and the guys on my pod were saying it was guys fighting over the phone. No big deal.

Then Busthead knocked a guy named Donald out cold with one punch inside of one of the cages outside, and was stomping hard him until the guards rushed out there to save him.

This was soon followed the next day by the unit Sergeant coming on the unit and going absolutely berserk at me for being out of my cell. He screamed at me and went all frothing at the mouth. I did not even have time to tell him how I could not push my own button in the control room, or that it was shower day and I was next man out to shower. I thought I was out for my cell as instructed by my routine. Fuck that shit. I had a chance to say nothing as he grabbed me by the throat and pinned me up against the cage of the day-room and choked the shit of me.

I kept at first trying to stay passive, he was so short that it was not a great grip that he could get on my neck to begin with and yet that just pissed him off more. As two of his officers rushed in to get some of what he was having, he grabbed me by the hair and flung me in the cell with a kick to my back for good measure.

I was so pissed off that I had this done to me because of a button being pushed too soon on the pod. What the fuck?

So, I am sitting on the bed a bit shook up and really angry while being "cackled on" by Bobby laughing over how I had my hair pulled so hard. His pal Dave got on his door next to him and was doing all that he could to keep his nose in Bobby's butt crack. He made sure of it by making it seem that every one of Bobby's sarcastic comments about me getting choked on by Sgt Rage was oh so clever and funny!

Oh they loved this chance to make each other feel so happy as a couple, they were going to cherish this moment for ever and ever...

I did not bother with retorts. I knew by the way everyone was acting that this shit was escalating more and more. I was not going to have to say anything to have someone to be combative with me, it was here all day and by all parties involved.

This is where it turned for me I think. I said to myself that day, that if I was not going to be able to get through being on this unit without being drug down into the gutter-brawls and such, then so be it. I tried for so many years to be passive. I just let a little prick of a man choke me when I could have whipped his ass all day long. That is so humiliating when you know you can best a man physically, but because of his absolute power over you, you have to let him act above you abusively.

I decided that I was going to only take so much shit before I finally let loose on someone. I just hated thinking of telling my parents how I tossed away any hopes we all had with a new set of criminal charges from this place.

I decided that if all of these crazy bastards were feeling like it was time to do whatever they wanted to me, that I was not going to take much more of it from here on.

I am so sad to say that during this brief period, that I went a little dark minded like this. I was just told that all of the biological evidence from my Death Row murder conviction case was destroyed, so I honestly believed that I was going to die there in that miserable hole.

Now, as much as I would like to claim that I had this all planned out, the truth is that what happened from here all unfolded because of "others" really, and what they did to one another mostly from it. I just kind of helped see that it happened I guess.

I was willing to do whatever I had to do to keep all of the other maniac killers on my pod all aiming their scorn at one another. It was easy to manipulate most of them for how they are wired mentally.

The fact that I had studied forensic psychology helped me to identify many traits of these men, and I would then play upon their weaknesses or strengths from this knowledge.

I worked diligently to be able to look at others closely in a mental perspective as they lived around me, all for the simple act of survival it provided me from my studies. I learned to use my skills to charm, cajole, or bully them into malleable partners in my unit. It was a lot of work at times, and there were some wasted cases like Roland whom you knew it was pointless to try this with.

But I worked it day and night. That was my "thing", or that was my technique to living with these men.

Good thing for me personally was "size and history of violence" matters. I had by this point survived many battles with others in the past. Because I was big enough to give them all they wanted, most men left me alone. Some of the past opponents had very big reputations as brawlers too. For this history of fighting them alone, the men now around me knew that I was not someone that was going to let you walk all over me.

That whole "Guards on inmate shit" with Sgt Rage gabbing me does not count, as a man in prison has the right in other prisoners eyes to simply not want to give up his life for a silly moment. No man wants to get new charges keeping him there forever either. That is taken as is *his* business. Let another inmate do the things that a guard tries on you, and that is when you have no choice but to act like nothing matters and hurt them.

Luckily for me, I was then struck by a series of events in which my physical self did not have to do much at all to do with my efforts to take out 2 of my enemies at once. I liked how this one was offered up to me...

In Pittsburgh Penitentiary the Death Row men were taken out of this 5 story high building and across the compound to the main visiting area for visits.

There they were put behind a 10 foot security glass enclosed section within the main visiting room, Inside of which had metal stools and telephones mounted on one long counter. Behind the thick security glass there were a series of 5 stools and 5 phones over each stool.

This is where you as a Death Row inmate get to be brought into what looks like an aquarium of sorts for visitation. You are the animal in the exhibit for all the normal visitors and children to see you inside of while seated inside this glass box.

Of course this was all inmate labor built and was the shoddiest set of phones you can use for visiting. All of the phones were connected to a security booth hidden within the walls of the visiting room, complete with a 2-way mirror fitted on it's door. This was where a hidden guard listened in on your conversations on each phone. It was the most awkward place to see your family as you heard 2, 3, or even 4 inmates on your side of this big glass enclosure all shout answers to unheard things being spoken to them into their phones. You have to work hard to try to blot it all out and focus on what you hear on a tinny phone line set right before you. Invariably you find yourself shouting too.

Now a lot of the times, if it is just 1 or 2 guys on these phones inside the visiting room at once it is better to deal with. The only problem is that sometimes the guard in the hidden booth leaves ALL of the lines open, so everyone using a phone then hears all of the other conversations from all the lines at once. This is annoying at the best of times, and is the one thing that lead to so much shit for me to have to then deal with on my unit later.

It all started with Rump being pulled out for a visit. He got searched and dressed and left the unit with "Frick and Frack".

Oh man, these were the 2 guards who's job it was floated around the jail, taking men from our unit (or other disciplinary units under our floor at the top) out to visits or hospital, or court processing. They were two of the most "fuck with your mind" guys ever. Both huge, both white, and both wired-for-combat is how I describe them. Push a panic button for help anywhere in the prison and these 2 guys light up like zoo animals who know it is feeding time!

They did all sorts of random things to men. They would get you into that slow ass elevator with them and on the way down, they did "body punches" on you to warm up their huge muscles.

"Frick and Frack", (who got their nicknames from both having the names "Frank" or somehow had Frank in it) were a bad combo to handle. These guys even made up their own moniker of a name of sorts, as they knew that this made them more menacing in jail. If you saw one of these men without the other guy, it seemed odd and you waited for the other to show up. So, together they put on their stage act for that one psychological effect that it had on men alone. It was borderline sociological in how they fed off of the other in heightened acts of "one upping" the other in the pain or torment of inmates.

I had no wants to be in their care at any time and I managed to make them both regret messing with me one day in a really fucked up way later on, all for how they treated me.

But right then I had to deal with Frick and Frack coming to take me out to a visit right after Rump left. I knew as I heard that I was being taken out there, how I already had that loud ass Rump to listen to over the phones while down there. I was just hoping there weren't any of the "shit tossers" from the mental ward under our unit in there as well. They even take their clothes off or touch themselves in the booth looking at females. Seriously, no hesitation or nothing to their doing it.

Nothing makes a visit suck worse than some guy who decides he saw a female "hot enough for me", (who was some innocent visitor out in the gen pop visiting area), and then he whips his dick out to start masturbating while inside the secure area. Really sad when you have to ask your mom or someone else who had driven for hours and hours to come see you, to please go to the toilets and or to look away. You then get to watch while the guards rush into the restricted visiting area and beat the guy with clubs before drag him off of the counter that he was standing on. They then come back in with an inmate wipe his semen off the visiting room glass...

When my pod opened and there stood these two guards before my cell, I went through all the same things I had to do in order for me to leave the unit. I handed over my clothes to be searched, I stood in clear view of both men as I showed my crotch and that ass-crack had nothing hidden in it by spreading myself open. I opened my mouth so they could shine a huge light inside of it to make sure I was not taking any handcuff keys or small notes with me out of the unit in my mouth.

I then put on each item of clothes which was handed back to me...undershorts, T-Shirt, socks, orange jumpsuit, and finally my rubber soled shoes back on correctly.

Once fully dressed, they put cuffs on me while wearing rubber gloves and they put a tether on the cuffs which one man held firmly as I exited my cell. Then they grab an arm each and they then led me off.

When I got on the elevator with these 2 men I had to put up with something close to 3 to 5 minutes of a creaking ride down that elevator. This one included both men munching a bag of potato chips which they had taken off of my desk at the last minute from inside my cell. They treated themselves to this gift when my cell was "searched" following my being taken out for visit.

As we rode along slowly down, they took turns crunching loudly in my face, all up close to my ear or right close to my eyes. After each time, one or the other man stuck his huge hand into the bag and filled his mouth with his haul. Oh they even burped in my face for me once or twice to share their potato chip smelly breath... (along with whatever breakfast they each had) all while smiling in my face. I silently stood there like I was some innocent commuter in a city. That I was on my train platform looking off into the sky and contemplating my day as if nothing bothered me...

In my mind though, I was thinking how these two jokers needed to be taken down a peg some day.

Now I am trying to not segue too far away from this trip on the elevator going to my visit this day, but you gotta know that if some dudes like this want to play with me..(like I am a "puppet"), then I was going to get them back if I could. Gotta make them respect me for not being a sap.

But it was gonna have to wait for another day for all of that fun, as I was on my way then to see my spiritual adviser who was bent on making me try to 'behave' while I was in this place. If she only knew what she was asking of me...

Now Frick and Frack were not allowed to just put me in the visiting room and vouch for me by saying they had already searched me. They had to hand me over to the visiting area officers so that they too could remove my chains and clothing. I then got strip searched all over by my new officers and put into "visiting" clothes that were a simple awful plum colored shirt and elastic waist banded trousers.

I was then put into a set of handcuffs in front that had the cuffs welded to a metal ring which was sewn into the front a 3 inch wide leather belt.

The two loose ends of the belt had a buckle and tongue holes in it with a small lock affixed to it that would be secured in the rear while I was wearing it. I could not undo the belt in any way once locked.

Then I was taken into the huge aquarium-like visiting room where there was only Rump sitting by the end stool alone, furthest from the door.

I sat down on my stool to wait for my spiritual adviser to come through the visiting room and over to where she could sit in front of me on a metal stool. I looked sideways at Rump and his visitor. I picked up the phone just to check and I could already hear them speaking so all of the lines were open. Shit.

Rump had gotten himself a "gal". He had a pen-pal who wrote him letters that was a woman from the local church group that she was part of. To Rump, this was surely heaven. He got to have time out of his cell with a very big breasted mature lady who was divorced and sweet by nature. While out there on a visit he was all aroused and doing his best to be charming...then he got to go back to his cell and furiously masturbate over it all in his mind. We would hear him in his cell whenever he came back from a visit talking to her out loud inside of his cell as if she were still present. He had cut a whole in his foam filled mattress and put her photo over it at eye level while laying on it himself. He would put butter around the hole and stick his penis in it and say he was "riding her"...He proudly told us all to listen to him as he was showing us how he would handle her in bed.

Trying very hard to not think of my man doing his "cowboy impersonation" in his cell at that moment as he was before me in the visiting room, I tried to focus on anything in the visiting room that I could lock eyes on. I did so trying to not trigger an attack from Rump as he is so mentally unstable. This guy was super strong when he flew into a rage and I was not going to play with him while he had his "boo" right in front of him. If that poor woman only knew about his mattress antics...

So, I am trying to keep my shit together as Rump does the worst whispering of sexy talk to his woman over the phone. All I can think about is what in the world the guard hidden in the 2 way glass booth was thinking about this guy talking sexy words.

Rump had his nose broken so much in the past that he had a really awful breathing noise. I sat there waiting for my visitor while thinking of how this must be the worst job ever in that 2 way mirrored booth if Rump has a hard-on in his trousers. Gotta be sick listening to his breathing as he is all excited sexually while he talks to that overweight woman (in the one-size-fits-most-dining-room-tables kind of0 dress that she was wearing. I tried really hard to keep my silly ass mind from not trying to conjure up whether or not Rump mentioned his drinking habits, or how he liked to sleep in bar toilets. I often wondered how these men told folks about their murder convictions like this.

Finally, I saw my spiritual adviser coming over and I smiled like I was finally seeing someone sane in the midst of this fucked up place. She sat down and looked at me really oddly. I was wearing a mix of "help me" and "you are not going to believe this shit" looks on my face. As I stood there at the phone I did that thing where I invited my visitor to note who we were sharing the phones with that day by casting my eyes to my right.

I tried to get her to look over to where Rump sat and then I raising my eye brows a bit.

My Spiritual adviser, not being as fearful of letting things slip, made herself look in that direction a little too obvious. She did not recognize the man on my side of the glass partition being Rump, but she sure eyed his visitor up. She looked quizzically at me and I did that whole "I wanna tell you, but I have a 800 Gorilla sitting beside me" look. That look that says "This guy is liable to snap at any minute and beat me around the room like a piece of luggage he if found me mocking his girl".

So, like the stupid mother fucker that I am, I mouthed the numbers "81" to her. She looks at me like I lost my mind. So, I tried a second and even more stupid looking try at mouthing the numbers "EIGHTY ONE"! Then I looked at people staring at me while I was standing there holding a phone at my waist...

In what must have looked to visitors behind my spiritual adviser who were looking in my direction as a man screaming loudly at her, I gave a shake to my head and gave up. I sat down in a slump when I realized that I looked like a maniac who was loudly yelling "81" to my visitor, when in fact I was not making any sound at all.

Then, like an child who tastes some new drink, my spiritual adviser finally twigged on to what I was saying. Her face lit up all brightly remembering me previously telling her how Rump had an IQ of just 81. She sat bolt upright with her eyes all alight just as I realized then that she was going to speak into a phone that I knew Rump was going to hear her speaking into!

As soon as I saw that she understood what I had tried to do to point out who we were next to, I should have put my fingers to my lips right then. I should have done that eye pleading thing with her to keep her mouth shut and that I knew how *she* understood the gag.

And just as I tried to shut her down, sure as shit she said; 'Oh, *that* 81'!!!

Oh man, I did not even have to fully turn my head for Rump to pick up on the fact that we had just touched upon his most embarrassing moment. Let's see, how can I put this any other way, but to tell it like it happened...

It was three weeks before that very day that I spent hoping to God that Rump was not going to beat me like I was some bar tender, that I witnessed the craziest post-visit moment of any prisoner in jail. I can not even hope to make this up.

So, Rump is literally retarded. Now, according to the law, you have to have an IQ of 79 or less to be spared being executed. Rump got tested by the courts and he has an IQ of 81. I know this because when he came back from his visit with his attorney where he was told this information, the boy was was soooo happy.

He was on his door immediately calling out to Dave how he had just gotten a "play". He explained that he was getting off of Death Row for his brain score!

When I heard this shit coming out of his mouth, I dropped my book that I was reading and got on the door along with everyone else. Any news of one of us getting out of there stirred up two immediate responses: Anger and resentment. Anger that this one is getting out of here and you are not, and resentment because of things they start shouting like; 'You dead mother fuckers are all now *eating* it'! You know, those quaint hurtful parting shots which they take as they walk out of hell, all to make you pissed off one last time.

So, just as I was about to witness all these men get angry and want to see him dead, Rump went on and told us all how he was getting off of Death Row thanks to this wonderful "play" that his lawyers told him he had just gotten from the courts.

Rump stood at his door and said that the courts had a law that anyone who has "79" is allowed to go out to population. The way he simply said the number "79" I started to wonder if anyone bothered to tell him that it was his IQ score they were telling him of.

Well, it was indeed his IQ which he had learned shortly and bitterly thereafter. See, Rump was nearly all the way through with telling all how he had about a year left with us on the Row, because his lawyers said they filed the appeal for this matter when Bobby jumped on him viciously.

He started saying how stupid Rump was to not even know how he was showing us all what a lame brain that he was to be given "2 points" as a pass by the courts. Saying further how he was lucky how his IQ of being a retard was well earned. He summed it up with more cruel shit about Rump being technically a moron. He then lay into Rump with how he was fuckin' brain dead anyway. Bobby totally humiliated him for five good minutes like that.

Ever since that day Rump was gunning for Bobby, but that bastard was so huge that Rump wouldn't take him on unless he had a good enough weapon. They both hated one another and yet they also hung out together in day-room and did crazy shit like played cards together.

Bobby had dominance over him in that way, so it was a suck-up-to-the-beast, (while hating the beast) relationship which they had together.

Well, back in the visiting room where my visitor had just picked the giant scab off of my buddy Rump's IQ test debacle, things went bad really quickly. Rump stood up and looked at me with his best "You're gonna die bitch" glare poisonously aimed at me, then dropped the phone on the counter top. I gave him that look of: "What'? "I didn't do *shit* "?! in return, but he was too pissed off to give me a pass.

I kept my eyes on him as he kicked on the door of the visiting room to be let out of there. When they got him out of the booth, I looked at my visitor and said: "Nice one, you know I now gotta go fuck him up for this now, right'? She just shrugged like, "How could I know"?

So, with about an hour of the most awkward prison phone visiting time over, I then went back to the pod. On the ride up Frick and Frack were saying how Rump changed his mood on them on his return to the unit, and they then wondering aloud to me "who" or "what" could have made him quit his visit early with his church lady friend with the big tits...

The way they said it, they expected me to give it all up to them then and join in with their laughing at Rump. I had no time to feed them anything for use on Rump and anything about me now having issues with him. I was trying to count how many paid envelopes I had in my cell right then...

Now, I knew Rump was going to come right after me. He was probably already back on the pod telling anyone who would listen to him, how I had just fucked his visiting time up. Oh I bet he did not mention that it was related to his IQ "thingie". But yeah, I knew he was back there telling the guys that I did some shit to mess with his people while they were there to see him.

When I got put back on the pod it had that "we just got done talking about this asshole" feel to it all. I knew my name was being used, and also I knew how Rump was fuming angry. It was then that I got the new guy who was put into Gary's old cell to be the bridge to my needs.

His name was "Yhati", and he was just a kid. Real name was KenYata. Just a slender light skinned black guy who was all of about 20 or so years old. He was on Death Row for a simple drive by shooting and the usual "hood" kind of crime. He had this over the top personality and he was so hyper active constantly.

So much so that Yahti was placed in Pittsburgh as they felt he was "too wild" for a more open setting any place else in the state.

Yahti wouldn't last long. His death is still one big fucked up mystery. He was too frail for this place I guess.

I liked Yahti personally, and we played chess together early on. I often joked with him about his hood life and how his game was much like a crack head. I felt a bit of a kinship with him as we both were basically children at that time of our lives when we were each put on Death Row.

Other than his not wanting Roland to be his new sex partner, (which he made clear right off to him) Yahti was "neutral" to everyone on our pod. He wasn't old enough to be in the mix too much yet. He kind of was untouchable anyway, what with him being a member of the "Junior Black Mafia" of Philadelphia.

There were like 4 or 5 of the head members scattered on Death Row from this notorious gang, and they did not let anyone mess with one of their foot soldiers. Yahti had check like that.

So basically Yahti could play with Bobby or any of the others verbally, all while knowing that none of them would kill him.

He wise-cracked his way along each day and no one better mess with him about it either.

Now I knew that Yahti had just come back from time spent down in the county jail. This meant that he had a gut full of balloons with weed or coke in them. He "muled" regularly for the bosses in the gang like this, and this too gave him sway in the unit over others. I figured that since Rump was broke, whereas I had a bunch of paid envelopes in my cell, that I could get him "baited" enough to get him off of me. I needed to get him to lose sight of wanting me dead from the visiting room incident while I then fed him someone else to focus his anger on.

So, I called over to Yahti loudly and I got him on his door to hear me. I told him that I had 300 paid envelopes and "could he hook me up"?

Yahti told me he had me covered. It was then that Rump, hungry to get some weed out of it, called over to me that he would move it on his homemade string line, moving it to me from Yahti's cell over to mine. We really did not need his help but he was ingratiating himself into the move as I wanted so I let him. We agreed to let him pass the envelopes back to Yahti for us as well. I smiled as I knew he wanted in so he could have something for his involvement.

I then said loud enough for anyone who Rump had been bitching to about me, all about my messing his visit up by saying:

'Hey man, sorry about that shit downstairs, I told that Bitch she ain't cool for doing that on a visit'!

Rump chimed right in and agreed that "my visitor" was now the one who had fucked things up, and how he was seeing me as a pal again for apologizing to him.

I got into my role more then, saying how him and me were still cool and that I really told that"bitch" who came to see me today that they had to go! I even said that was why I came off my visit early too, as I wanted to set things right out of respect for Rump.

Rump warmed up to the way I was selling it for him then. He just knew he was getting some of that weed from Yahti now...

So, I sent the 300 paid envelopes that I placed in a small pretzel bag (that was sealed inside two bags within that one) and all attached to a string in front of my door at the floor. I then sent it over so that Rump could snag it. Rump then flung it along the floor to Yahti.

The bag is always needed in case some rotten bastard in the cells between you all takes that moment to toss a cup of piss (or piss *and* feces mixed up in a cup) on the floor in an effort of ruining your envelopes or other items.

Once Yahti got paid, he sent his line over with 2 or so grams of weed in it. Rump got the balloon in and he waited.

And perfectly on cue, I said: 'You take half of that now Rump and you can pay me back later'.

I knew and that he knew he wasn't paying me shit for the weed. He was gonna take nearly all of it too. He played his retarded part perfectly at times like that. He made a big show of sending me over the rest after he did all this taking his share, all so that everyone thought he hadn't ripped me off in a petty way.

I know this is insane, that he needed to demonstrate like this by showing everyone that he wasn't a total asshole to me, but this is the world that I lived in.

I then heard about 6 to 8 flushes of his toilet in Rump's cell, (where Rump took a puff on a "one-hitter", which is a home-made pot smoking pipe, all while standing over his toilet) so he was blowing the smoke into his commode as it flushed to suck away the smoke.

By now he was fucked up I was betting.

About 5 minutes later that Rump began making noises in his cell that were really strange.

It was the sound of "headphones-on-his-head while-singing" that we soon heard. They are weirder than others you usually hear when someone doing this when it is a Death Row prisoner like Ronnie who is fucked out of his face on drugs. Especially so when he is singing only half of the words to songs which he is listening to. It was all very passionately done at a emotionally charged high pitch is why it got so weird.

Then after a break at times in this performance of singing, Rump got to sobbing while singing and he sometimes starts crying over the musical words. It is like some really messed up opera act where you know this is all shit now, and you want it all to stop. The fact that Rump loved county music made it really fucked up, as you heard him in this case getting all emotional about some dog dying in the song...

You laugh if others are laughing, (as I was then) but don't be the one laughing when he takes the headphones off and he hears you saying shit about him.

That is exactly what Bobby was doing when he was wondering aloud to Dave about how; 'I wonder if Rump is crying because he was thinking about how he used to be the dog in that cage that had died in the song'... Followed further by;

'Or you think it is because he wants to fuck that dog in the cage like he wants to do to his lady-friend with the big tits who comes see his sick ass on visits'?

That was exactly what Bobby had just finished yelling a bit too loudly to Dave when Rump went from singing his heart out, to full on screaming at Bobby in response to hearing this taunt. Oops. I guess Bobby did fall for my set up.

I shoved my face into my pillow while laughing hysterically in bouts of laughter as Bobby rose to the bait from Rump. He and Rump went to work on each other about mothers with farm animals with all manner of shit they said about one another s' family members included.

It got heated quickly after that first round of insults about each other having "whores" or "faggots" for parents. They then began escalating things further by making it known to us all that as soon as the doors popped open again, that it was gonna be "World War 3 Bitches"!

When I saw that Rump and Bobby were going to go at it physically, I leaped into it there and then. I took up Rump's side of this incident by getting on my door and shouting at Booby too. I said Bobby wasn't nothing but a "big fat bitch", and then I added how Dave was his "old lady" in prison and how Dave loved to suck his ass any chance that *she* got.

That got both Bobby and Dave both into it then, and I smiled slyly as I kept setting the stage for what I wanted next to happen. I kept pumping Rump up by saying things like: 'Fuck them Rump, they are just jealous because you and me got down with Yahti's good shit to smoke'!

Rump kept at it until it got boring for everyone after 20 minutes, and we all settled down for the weekend.

You could smell the simmering and seething hate all inside of that place for the next 2 days. I kept making sure that I laughed coarsely a whole lot that weekend too, just to keep them angry at what I found so funny.

Bobby helped later on Sunday night when he came to the door remembering something which he had forgotten earlier during the shouting on Friday...

Out of no where, about 9:pm Sunday night Bobby
started calling Rump "Captain Pooh" over and over in a
sing-song voice. This was when I knew things were going
to be turned into a bloodbath on the following Monday
morning. I knew things were for real when day-room
finally came about after Bobby started to really
humiliate him with this next bit.

Poor Rump. He was asked to bring back a dozen or so
balloons once, from a trip to the main prison he had
taken. It was arranged by others in gen-pop and all he
had to do was follow instructions. He agreed to pick the
balloons up at the hospital during his post-hernia
surgery check-ups which he needed. All he had to do
was swallow them there once an inmate passed them
to him, come back to his cell and crap them out.

Now Rump being the foolish person that he is, told us
all how he had a package inside of his guts that he
wanted out of him just as soon as he was back on the
pod from the hospital that evening.

All night he talked bout how he couldn't wait to shit
them balloons out and get high. It was Dave who told
him that if he was so anxious to get them out, how he
should try to do enemas to help him.

Rump said in a typical retard fashion that he had enough enemies and we all laughed at his dumb ass for misunderstanding Dave. Then Dave told him that he would make "something" that Rump could use to get the drugs out and to ignore us dicks for laughing like that. We all waited for whatever we would see slide out of Dave's cell for Rump then...

So, out comes a half squashed shampoo bottle which looked to have had an ink pen stuffed into the spout opening. It had some white string holding it securely to the top of the bottle I could see. I surmised that this object was going to be shoved up Rump's ass after water was to be put into the bottle, to then somehow try to flush out his intestines.

Well, being as it was nearly 10:pm and we were due for out shift change of guards, he should have just chilled. This was going to be a time when the only guard on duty makes his lone pass on the unit to see if all 48 of his children are in their cells. That one chore of his done, the guard usually went to sleep in the control booth for 8 hours. Rump could have waited another 10 more minutes or so, but retards don't have normal brains to let them do things others would obviously do.

This fucking idiot was on his knees inside of his cell with an ink pen shoved up his ass (that was now attached to a bottle with a quart of water inside) when the pod doors kicked open.

Now, we all knew that Rump was doing this shit inside his cell, so of course Bobby tried to stop the guard and talk to him about some request slips which he said that he needed. The guard blanked Bobby and slammed the outer door on the first side of the pod and kept right on walking...

He was ten steps along when we all heard: 'WHAT THE MOTHER FUCK ARE YOU *DOING* INMATE'?!

The passing guard observed Rump was on all fours with the bottle sticking out of his ass with one hand holding the bottle, as the other hand was trying to squirt water up into his ass. That was when he yelled so loud like that for us all to hear. Of course in a panic Rump then snapped the pen off in his asshole trying to yank it out.

Rump began screaming in agony from his ass being ripped. He kept yelling that his ass was bleeding and the guard broke into hysterical laughter as he pulled out his Walkie-Talkie to begin calling for the other guards in the unit. He shouted for them to get up there on his floor now.

He poured it on too, saying over the system that he just found a guy jamming a bottle up his asshole!

We were all laughing so hard on the pod as they had to put Rump on a gurney and roll him out to the same hospital that he had just come from, only to now get a pen out of his rectum. They of course also got the drugs out of his stomach once they figured out what he was doing in his cell. They put him in a sealed room for a week that had nothing in it but a bucket. Rump told us later that when he shit the balloons out, how he broke his stitches that were in his asshole.

He did brag that despite this all that nasty mess though, how he even tried to break open a shitty, blood-soaked balloon to eat some of the dope before they took it all from him.

Rump was dedicated like that I guess...

Look, I knew right then back to that night, after Bobby was calling Rump names to remind him of the hospital incident, how either Bobby or Rump was probably dying on Monday morning. I even bought Rump half a bag of hooch off of George, the guy who bartered for everyone's fruit, all just to make wine from this material inside of his cell.

George would starve himself by trading all his food away for a few apples here, or a half-finished grapefruit there, all so that he could drink hooch.

I knew that he always had a batch cooking. I figured that since Rump was definitely going to lose against this giant, why not buy the man one last drink on a Sunday night? I even sent over the last of the weed from Yahti so that he could sing all night long and really piss Bobby off even more.

What Bobby and no one else knew then, as this all went down, was that I was working on Rump in the vents between our cells the whole time. I told him that we should just take Bobby out together on Monday when we both go in the day-room as a team. I said that I had a nice weapon that I was gonna use on Bobby to help get this over with finally. I lied of course.

I told him that I also had a metal lock left over from my cell property locker, and that I managed to sneak it back to my cell from the property room when we first came into the pods.

I told Rump that I had put the metal lock into 2 pairs of socks, tying it around tight so as to make it into a 'lock-in-a-sock' weapon. I said how he could bash Bobby's brains out with this thing while I then stabbed Bobby to death with my prison "shank".

Rump was all excited to finally have someone help him to murder humans now, as in the past he had to do it all by himself I guess.

He kept saying "yeah" over and over, each time that I told him how big and sturdy that my shank was which I had made for us to use.

So, I sent the "lock in the socks" to Rump late into the night on Sunday, slipping it on a line which I had made all very discreetly to him. I made sure to pump him up some more then with a note included with the lock that read; "Bobby sucks dick"!

I knew that I couldn't risk big words inside of my note written to Rump, so I stuck to the ones which I knew that Rump understood easily. I heard him say "Yeah!" one more time after he had read my comment about Bobby's oral skills. I then went over and lay in my bed while waiting for the excitement of the morning to come around. It was like waiting for the most fucked up Christmas morning ever...

So the execution of my little staged play went like so:

First, the Sergeant came around and opened all the slots and took names for who was going out to the yard or day-room for exercise.

Bobby was ever so eager to sign up for day-room, all while making sure that Rump heard him say it very loudly. This was the challenge being thrown down.

Rump waited for Dave to say that he was going to the yard next. I was thinking maybe because Dave was so deeply tied to big Bobby, that was going to be reacting emotionally whenever his man was involved in fights like this. It was Dave who got very upset whenever it happened, (like any wife does), when they are watching their partner knife a fellow human right before them.

Rump then said in his best cowboy voice ever; 'Yup', 'I am going to the day-room too'!

Sgt. Rage did not twig on to any of this challenge between Rump and Bobby being laid down, so he just moved on. I then of course said that I was going to day-room as well next. I knew that Rump was all pumped up by this act (he knocked all softly on my cell wall letting me know he had heard me sign up for day-room) as he must have been thinking it was now clearly us as a team who were against "Mr. Big Bad Bobby". This was all now set to kick off in about an hour's time...

Then comes Poor George who *had* to go and sign up for day-room on this go around. No one else wanted day-room but him on that side. Idiot.

I was thinking that he really chose a bad day to come out and try to get on the phone. I mean, this was clearly going to be a kill zone so what was he thinking when he did this?!

I even meant to send him a note to tell him to skip the day-room that morning but I forgot, alright?

Now I know that I let that poor, crippled, brain-damaged man go right in there that day when I knew what was coming. I am not proud of it. I am sorry, but that was not my main focus of the moment.

I actually needed George to at least *sign up* for the day-room so that they would start at Bobby's cell and finish with George being pulled out slowly in his wheel chair. The rest was on him for going out of his cell I told myself.

The guard in the control booth popped the pod doors on time at 9:am. The guards entered the pod and went right to left, taking Bobby first to day-room. He sat at the table far back from the door with a deck of cards in his hands. Then Rump went in there to join Bobby in day-room.

When when the guards got to my door, I yelled out that I was 'on the toilet'!

I then told them to pass me over today because my stomach was bothering me.

They then picked George out of his cell. Once he was done going into the day-room the guards then left our pod so that they could go around to the other pod next to ours, to get that 1 more guy needed to fill the 4 slots of day-room time. Now was my chance.

Rump was standing while facing my cell and was looking at me for an answer as to why I let him go alone into the day-room with Bobby. Clearly we were not doing this as team USA.

I ignored all that and kept mouthing the words 'Get him'! in response to his looks. I was looking out of my door at him, all the while making mean faces at Rump to spur him on to take action.

Bobby was sitting at the table with the deck of cards in his hands while shuffling them slowing. He watching Rump from behind as he stood facing me. I watched as George asked if Bobby minded if he used the phone. Bobby waived his hand to George like a peasant being granted his passage, so then Georgie-boy nervously backed his wheelchair towards the phone, keeping his eyes on Bobby to see if it was a joke or not this time...

As George wheeled himself backwards towards the phone, I nodded at him and Rump chose that moment to strike. He stuck his right hand inside of his jumpsuit while facing me to fish out his weapon. He began to wrap the athletic socks around his fist. Then he began pulling the lock-in-a-sock weapon out of his clothes like a big white floppy worm that was coming out of his belly.

He looked at me one last time (with that "here goes *nothing*" look on his face), then he spun without warning while then swinging the weapon at Bobby's face. Rump cracked Bobby square in the top of his head with the lock wrapped up in a pair of socks just as hard as he could.

Blood shot all over the glass of the day-room behind Bobby then, as blood began to also run down Bobby's face from where his head had just been gashed open ABOUT 4 inches wide from the metal lock. Rump swung again, and again, as he cracked Bobby right on top of his head 2 more times with that thing.

Bobby then started to rise up slowly out of his chair as he shook off the first blows from the attack. As he did so, he pulled out a big ass home-made shank from within his jumpsuit.

Bobby wobbled backwards as Rump swung a huge arching attempt that missed. Instead of hitting Bobby, the wild swing shattered the window of the pod security glass with his weapon.

The Lock went through the glass and was ripped out of the socks that were holding it, only to then fall into the hallway outside on the floor. Rump was left to stare at this useless pair of empty socks now wrapped on his hand after he missed.

That was just as Bobby took him by the throat with his giant fist and pinned Rump against the mesh wire of the day-room walls and began stabbing him.

Bobby began to stab Rump over and over in the belly while holding him there like a rag doll. I know that it was like 20 or 30 times that I saw him stab Rump in the belly, and yet Rump was still standing upright. He was fighting to get free of that fist which was locked around his throat as the guards came on the pod and sprayed both guys in the face with the tear-gas. They then entered the day-room to beat them both to the floor while they cuffed each one behind their backs.

George had been knocked over in his chair from the scuffle and he even had Bobby step on him once as he tried to drag himself clear of the brawl. It was all over in about 3 minutes total.

It was so chaotic with the tear gas soon making everyone sick instantly inside, that it was like we all had gotten involved.

It just went on and on as they drug Bobby out of day-room while clubbing the shit out of him before tossing him in his cell. They then came back into the day-room and began dragging Rump out by the feet and thumping him hard as well for his part in this.

As they drug Rump past my cell, I saw why he survived 20 or 30 stabbing attempts.

He had magazines taped to his body! I thought he looked a bit chunky that day I said to myself then. Lucky bastard had taped all these fishing magazines around his body, using it like body armor to stop a blade. That's why he did not get butchered by that shank that Bobby had held in his giant fist and used on him.

The only guy on the pod who had fishing magazines sent to him every week was Dave.

Don't ask me why a guy like Dave would do that to Bobby, where he loaned Rump his favorite fishing mags for him to protect himself in battle. I just believe what I saw on Rump. I know damn right well that Rump was too dim to make that move of making body armor for himself as well.

So Dave, you hated having to suck up to Bobby all along it seemed. I feel ya, sir, I feel ya...

I stood at my cell door and I laughed and I laughed over how I had just gotten two of the sickest monsters to battle it out for me. I thought myself oh so clever to have them do my bidding on one another like that.

And all the while that I stupidly laughed at my nasty deeds, there was one person there who had heard it all play out before them. They also figured out what I had done exactly to both Bobby and Rump. That was Roland of course. He was now going to make his moves on me for it.

As I stood there enjoying my moment of triumph, he decided that he was going to give me a taste of how it felt in manipulating others by the master himself. He stood there thinking that this was how to exactly do me in. I figured that he was growing tired of waiting to get me by his own acts, so I had just showed him a game now that he really liked to try on me.

In the aftermath of the battle, Bobby and Rump got 90 days disciplinary time each. They had all of their possessions taken as Rump got moved out of his cell, and into another one that was away from us all.

He was soon to get off Death Row for having mental retardation and got to go out into gen-pop where he was to serve his natural life sentence there.

I went back to my own handling of my own troubles and sat in my cell waiting for one of the others to try to kill me. It was business as usual after that fight. All they did was shuffle a guy or 2 around, then wait for things to settle down just a bit before they thought of something new for us.

5. 'The Way I was Prey'

3 times a week I put myself at risk by showering on the pod by going into the area know as "shower-room". This was that one enclosure which has the shower curtain on the wire across the front. Because I always wore eye glasses due to being nearsighted, I was truly vulnerable when I washed my hair. This is nerve wracking and you have to have big balls to ignore everything else to do this without showing fear. I always wore shower shoes with a good grip on my feet, and I never took off my boxer shorts while washing my body. I washed them while on me.

I always shaved in the shower and not my cell. There was no point in trying to look at a piece of metal while doing this act, as it made you dizzy without your glasses on looking at blurred metal of a security mirror.

So, I learned to shave with my eyes closed in the shower while using my hand as a guide on my face as I did this. Many years of this and I can shave perfectly without seeing my face once.

My main hater of a guard was an ex-cop. This former police officer who had gotten himself fired for being a drunk was a nasty piece of work. Irish and a mixed heritage of European descendants, he had gray hair and a squat body. He stood about 6 foot tall. He was thick and his body was that of a drunkard with the extended belly and bowed back. Loud and nasty tongued when he did speak to you, he thought nothing of getting on the intercom and reading guys criminal cases out for the whole pod to hear. He would cut the phone off to your mom when he felt like it, he burnt mail that you waited weeks for it to arrive... he just loved mind fucking guys.

I did not know it at the time, but Roland had made a new pal out of this guard. Roland was working him good behind my back. They laughed at jokes together and Roland for whatever reason, soon got extra law library time each week so that he could go have sex with our new pod mate.

"Marty" was this madman's name who had be chosen to replace Rump on our pod. This guy was a little dark haired maniac who was about 5 foot 5 and weighed no more than 110 pounds. Marty was the white boy psycho who went into a bank near his home town in a central part of Pennsylvania with another guy and began to massacre everyone inside of the bank on the spot.

Marty was deeply saddened that his co-defendant and also his lover of the time had turned states evidence against Marty. He went mentally dark after he had his heart broken by this act of betrayal at trial by his co-defendant they said.

Now Marty was crazy as anyone Ise whom I had ever met, and he loved to think that he was somehow not one of us "regular guys" on Death Row. He was full on "America is the land of greatness" in speeches out of his cell, all while he was being executed by America for being hated by his blessed country. He was so twisted in his mind that when Bill Clinton was elected as a democrat to be President, Marty was such a staunch republican, that he went mental in his cell and said that no "democrat" had the right to execute *him*!

So on and on it went. Roland was living it up well now all because he had gotten really good at sucking up to this one guard. Thus he was having his new lover Marty come out of his cell with him to able to have "romantic times" in the law library several times a week. I could care less about that aspect.

Then came the next parts of how this was all to do with me...

Roland was going out to the Sergeant's office and he was feeding them all of the intelligence about who was doing what on our pod.

Of course this snake fed them the truth to start off with, only to add in all of the lies that he needed to spread to the guards to mess anyone up whom he hated on.

If there was anything which Roland knew about or learned of that was going inside on the pod, it soon got found out about by the guards. He got the guards to search my cell when he saw me get a package in from a guy named "Lonnie" which was the worst one of his tricks that he did to me.

That snitch-move of his got me 60 days without my TV and radio, and nor was I even allowed any books to read for 2 months. That was dreary. What really hurt me is that one shitty act is what got my friend Lonnie killed.

This is some strange shit, but it is all there in news papers to read and see how it is all true...

Lonnie, whom everyone called "Jihad" was from West Philly. A light skinned, easy smiling kind of guy, he was sent to Death Row back in 1984. I met Lonnie in Holmesburgh prison back in Philly while I was down there for court.

He and I for some reason got along right off. When I saw Lonnie had landed on Death Row in Huntingdon prison 2 years later beside me, I then agreed to help do his legal work with him.

With me and another guy helping him, Lonnie managed to get his Death sentence taken off of him for this effort. He was given life without parole for a robbery-homicide that he did of a store owner.

Since I helped Lonnie back then on Death Row, he was always a loyal friend for what I did for him. While he was in Huntingdon and out in general population there he used to send me a dozen donuts each month from his "lifer's package". This was a prison thing that he was allowed to participate in which allowed him to buy outside food for being in the Pennsylvania "Lifers' program". I made good money off of this treat each month, and he kept me afloat like that for a few years while I was there. Then Lonnie got moved to Pittsburgh and I lost contact with him.

I got word sent to me by Lonnie one day in 1996 that he was back from court recently, and that he had heard I was in the security unit. He had been doing time with one of my friends named Norman who told Lonnie that I got shipped to Pittsburgh the year before. Lonnie wanted to know if I was 'okay" mentally, or if he could do anything for me.

This message being passed was his way of staying true to the ones whom he had bonded with over the years.

The message from Lonnie was given to me by one of the gen-pop prisoners who came up each week to cut hair for the security unit prisoners. This job was fought for and given to only those guys who had serious pedigrees. Not by the staff mind you. You did not even apply for this job because it was off limits in jail to any guy not seriously connected. Why? Because so many important messages were sent by them verbally or written, to the leaders of gangs who were serving disciplinary time in the "hole" or were those on Death Row.

When I heard how Lonnie was in the same jail as me then, I sent him a message to send me any kind of package of whatever he could spare. I needed it so that I could make money now that I lost all of my hustles at Huntingdon. He knew how I quit getting high years ago, but I had no qualms about making money for cosmetics and food, or especially for postage-paid envelopes.

The only thing was, I had to go out and get it. That meant that I had to get a trip to the hospital set up. That in itself was very hard for me as I had already escaped prison once.

The only thing that I could do then was come up with internal bleeding or severe stomach issues to get out of my cell. I had to contrive and use symptoms correctly of some form of internal injury so then I could get to be taken out to the Hospital to meet Lonnie.

I waited a week following my getting that message before I sent word to Lonnie to be ready about the last weekend of that same month. I then got everything together that was going to let me get through this (and do so in a way that no one wanted to handle me physically while I tried this move) as well.

I purchased 4 bags of gum drops along with 6 bags of BBQ potato chips from the commissary a week before I put my plan to work. I then began to starve myself on a Monday, hoping that by Thursday evening of that same week, how I was going to be ready to be taken out of that cell and over to the Hospital.

On Wednesday of that week I went to the shower and I cut my leg with the razor above the ankle of my right leg by moving the safety razor side-ways on my skin until blood came out good.

I then put a wash cloth on it and soaked up the blood without letting it get too diluted in the shower.

When I had a lot on the cloth, I folded up my bloody wash rag and put it into the clear plastic soap dish which I had with me. I even did as best that I could to get more blood into the dish with the cloth by scraping my leg with the edge of the soap dish before closing it up.

Once I had a nice amount of my own blood stashed away, I washed my leg off, put a white sock on both of my feet with my shower shoes on to go back into my cell.

Next, I did my best to make sure that the cuts healed by not moving much. Then on Thursday morning I began eating the gum drops and BBQ chips at the same time. Being so hungry did not help this awful mix taste any better than the gooey candy melting in my mouth over sour BBQ.

There I sat with a plastic cup of water, eating gum drops and BBQ potato chips for an hour. I ate every last bit of these nasty things, and I then went to sleep right afterwards to let it all ferment in my guts over night.

On Friday morning I told Sgt. Rage that I was too sick to eat and that I had blood in my urine. Then, when he tried to talk to me like I was an asshole at my door during head count, I told him how I was unable to focus and stumbled back to bed.

I told Sgt. Rage to come into my cell and look at my toilet while I acted all faint. He demanded that I step back up to the door to be cuffed as he called for my door to be opened. Then once another officer came over to be with him, he went into my cell.

I was holding his movement up for yard and day-room sign ups and there had better been real blood in the toilet he said, or I was going to bleed it right then from my face if there wasn't any there.

When he came in the cell, he saw the red droplets on my white boxer shorts right below my penis. He saw the droplets on the toilet which I had dripped out of the soap dish and onto the rim of it to make it look good. Then he looked down into the bowl and he saw all that blood and my urine mixed together. He said to the officer; 'Get this idiot to the Hospital, this fucker is dying or *some* shit'!

I put on my best "Oh shit this is *bad*"! look on my face. while I then went over gingerly and sat down slowly on the bed with the guard holding my arm. Ten minutes later, I was in the loving embrace of Frick and Frack. They were not happy to be moving me this early in the morning before day-room time, even before when their first cup of coffee was to be enjoyed.

I really put on the show for Frick and Frack, as I was wearing only boxer shorts then. I handed out all of my clothes to them as I groaned like a sad ghost. As I did this, I began forcing myself into farting as much as I could. The stench from BBQ chips and gum drops is putrid and nasty. It began fuming out of my cell soon. It was making me sick, so I knew that Frick and Frack were instantly disgusted.

They tossed my clothes to me and they got my door opened and yanked me out in a flash. I kept acting all weak in the knees as I kept hunching over in made up pain, while moaning to them that I could not hold it any longer...

All the while I was doing this act before them internally I was trying hard to make myself shit my pants. By the time they got me to the elevator in this slow procession, I was letting out one steady stream of the worst gas ever from my ass.

They put me against the wall and said to me that if I did shit myself on the elevator how they were going to fuck me up good. I pleaded for them to please know how I was really sick, and this was real messed up with blood in my piss. I said that I couldn't help it. I even tried to make myself cry by thinking about Roland out in the woods beating my mother to death instead of one of those old ladies he killed out there.

When the elevator doors finally opened on the top floor and we all got on together, they pushed me to the back of the elevator with their clubs holding me there. They held me there as far away from them as possible as they then stood by the doors with their free arms folded over their noses like train robbers hiding their faces.

I did my best to push my guts really hard at that point and sure enough, I began to have diarrhea come out. I felt it all nasty and warm begin to run down my legs...

Both guards were getting physically ill from the stench then. I kept on trying to fart or shit myself over and over as best that I could so it was made worse for them too. It went on and on in that slow moving box of an elevator.

Frick and Frack were cursing me through the sleeves of their shirts that were held over their mouths the whole time. They were like frantic men who were dying of their own breaths as that elevator slowly went on down at a snails' pace. I never once broke character and I did my best to keep it together knowing this kind of trick got your brains beaten out. This was out-on-a-limb shit here folks, and get you don't play around for stuff like this to then joke.

Frick and Frack jumped out of the elevator minutes after we had all gotten on it. They kept spitting and gasping for air as they got off in an angry manner.

After they had sucked in enough new air to clear that nastiness out, they then turned back and grabbed my tether that was on my handcuffs and pulled me out violently by tugging on it it. I nearly fell at their feet then, and they were horrified that I was almost getting shit on them by touching them. They eased up a bit and let me get my feet under me.

We then in unison all did the nastiest walk of my life to that point, off across the prison grounds. We trekked over to the Hospital while shit ran down my legs the whole time.

The whole way there, they were swearing at me that if I did not die from whatever it was that in my guts smelling like that, how they were going to make me wish that I had died from it. Especially if I got *any of my* shit got on either one of them in the process.

I was taken to the shower rooms that were located inside of the Hospital wing and allowed to strip alone in the shower. No one wanted to come near me and smell me. I put everything in a pile that I was wearing as instructed and placed them in a garbage bag that I was given. I was issued new prison garments from the Hospital ward instead of my orange security ones. I was given paper slippers too, since my shoes were ruined with shit.

I was then placed into a secured room and hand-cuffed to the bed by one arm. I was on what was then the known as the surgery ward. I could not get the smell off of me from my BBQ potato chip shit-fest, nor could I get out of my mind how it felt to be covered in filth and made to walk. It was like someone had burnt a baby diaper full of shit from a child combined with take-away Indian food that was all mashed up inside of it. My nose was burning from it all...Spicy-turd smell is all I can say.

In time, I got a brief check-up from the nurse on duty who she said that the doctor would be around after a while to examine me.

I told her that I was feeling a lot better but that I was exhausted so I needed to sleep if I could. She said that she would let them know that. She said afterwards she would have the doctor come by when I was feeling better later on. The guard then un-cuffed me from the bed as per her orders. I rolled over and went to sleep.

All I had to do was wait it out in that bed, well past 3:pm when Frick and Frack left for the day. I would then have to be left here in the Hospital for the whole weekend.

Then all I had to do was wait for Lonnie to show up...

I managed to get through the doctors 2 :pm call by again making sure to fart as much as I could in that room before he entered. It's disgusting what I had to do, but I had to convince them that I had a serious intestinal virus or some other internal injury/ailment that would allow me to stay. I saw right away once again how no one wants to breathe the nasty stuff that I was putting out, as the doctor stood at the door with a surgeons mask held to his face while speaking to me about my symptoms.

I then described perfectly all of the symptoms of gastritis, or what could be a serious virus of the stomach.

As the doctor asked me if I had eaten anything that might have disagreed with my stomach, I told him that I had not eaten in days from the pain of my stomach. He looked down on my unit notes to see how they had noted on my prison records how the staff reported that I had not eaten since Monday on the unit. Boom, job done. Blood in urine was due to dehydration he said to me.

He closed that door as fast as he could after telling me how he was prescribing medications to help with what he thought for sure was a stomach virus. He signaled to the officer and nurse with him to note that I would be kept there for observation.

I smiled just a bit as I had done it perfectly. I got myself out of the unit and I had my boy Lonnie going to come over that Saturday to see me there. Lonnie actually worked there at the hospital as an orderly at the time so this was going to be real easy.

All I had to do after that happened was for me to make it back onto my housing unit without getting searched by Frick and Frack.

Lonnie showed up Saturday morning and I was on my door smiling at him through my door while being proud of myself for getting this far along into the plan. He said he would be back after breakfast to "run things down" for me...I did not know if I liked hearing this part, as it suddenly sounded a little fishy to me. When I looked at him like I was just here for a pick up of his package, Lonnie reassured me by saying 'It's cool, you just gotta help a brother out'. Upon hearing this from him I was like, "Oh no he did *not* just do this shit to me once I did all of this to get here"...

After I ate my first food in days that morning, my sore belly kept beating up on me for what I did to it with the gum drops and potato chips. I felt so awful from the gluten and sugar which I had consumed that my joints ached and I felt really slow witted too. Lonnie came by to collect the trays and clean up the floor that afternoon.

As he stood by my cell holding his mop, with me crouched down to look out of my pie hole, it was then that he told me that I was in for a treat which he had in store for me. I asked what was on the menu and he said: 'Oh the usual, but something *nice* too'.

Now I knew for sure right then that we had gone from Lonnie was "going to hook me up" (wherein we were both just going to have another moment of bros looking out for one another), to this new game of his.

I waited for Lonnie to show his hand.

'So listen Nicky-boy', he began... He followed with: 'I got you *right,* but I need a favor too'...(here it came, the Lonnie pitch)... I knew he was going to get me into some shit when he next spoke.

Without wanting to tell me that he had decided to actually use me, Lonnie told me how he was going to have to none the less have to use me for coming down there to the hospital.

It was all for him to make a nice bit of money off of me while pretending that he had something for me. He said that since I was willing to come down here anyway, what is the difference who was making money? You can imagine the expression I wore on my face upon hearing this shit.

I looked at him the same way in which anyone does when you just got handed the real item you thought you were buying. Here he was using me to take shit back inside the unit for probably the "Junior Black Mafia".

In reality though soon learned how it was for one of Lonnie's prison pals housed in the unit below mine just then, someone whom he owed money to. He flatly forgot all of his previous spoken words about this being all set up for *me*.

And all while he was now telling me how he none the less was "hooking me up" somehow. Yeah right, Lonnie.

So, basically whatever I was being "given" at the start of all this jailhouse bullshit, was now my risk-reward for taking things back to the pod for him. I knew that this would get me in serious trouble on the unit or even new criminal charges now. I looked at him a long moment and said: 'Wow *really*, Jihad'?

He said: 'Oh come on motherfucker, you act like you never did any *moves* before'! That was meant to remind me that I once ran a gambling operation previously, or how I used to sell schoolwork to gen pop guys who were too dumb to read, let alone pass college exams.

That all had nothing to do with Lonnie setting me up to take whatever he was making money off of on the unit now with me. The way he was putting pressure on me, I knew he was in deeply to somebody for a debt. I cut him a break and said: 'Okay road-dog, what we gotta do *this* time'? I then was told that I had a "belly pack" to take back. Oh shit.

If you melt plastic around items it molds them all tightly together. Take a yellow bin liner bag and melt it around several objects and then press them down to conform to your belly's shape by standing on them for hours. You try to make it crescent shaped so that you make a object that is mostly flat and mold-able to your midriff.

Whatever was going to be in the belly-pack was going to be worth a lot of trouble, as you hardly ever got anything big into the unit. All I could hope for was that there were no saw blades, handcuff keys, or shank blades for weapons making of any kind inside of this thing. Those are all new charges. Otherwise this was either going to be a small amount of grass and some notes for the top guys in the JBM and possibly cash too inside of the thing.

My job was to get the package back to the unit and send it unopened to the top guy in the "JBM".

He then was going to break it down into who gets what. I knew right then how I was going to get screwed over mostly, as once I let this thing out of my hands like that, it was gone for good.

I knew that I was not getting the same respect from those guys that Lonnie had for me. I weighed up my chances and thought about how I was being played in everyone's game. I just went along with it. Once I said how I was down with the plan, Lonnie got all brightened up. Lonnie said to me that he had to put things in play first, but that he had something "extra special" for me, just for doing his this huge favor for him.

I could imagine him coming back and saying some dumb shit about how I was gonna have to do some other dirty job, but he did not pull a lame move on me like that.

I had one of the best Saturday evenings of my life that day! It was going to be my only day to eat, as I had to get a concoction from Lonnie Sunday morning to take that was meant to give me the diarrhea again. I had no real hope of having the same terrible gas to go along with my trip back to my unit, as we were not getting any sweets and BBQ chips in the hospital. I figured that I was still pretty deadly enough with my farts that weekend no matter what, so all I had to do was take one more filthy shit encrusted walk back to my cell to be done.

Lonnie sent me over a Philly Cheese Steak sandwich from the kitchen and he added some fruit cups as well. I was living it up good then, with even some candy sent over in my dinner tray to boot.

At 10:pm that evening the night officer came by and left my pie-hole open without a word. I thought that was well odd but kept my mouth shut.

I was looking out of the pie-hole of my hospital cell for like 20 minutes when I had a big ass shock hit me.

There was Lonnie with the nurse in tow, and it was none other than the nurse who was hooked up with the same lieutenant from our unit! I was so stunned that I just stood like an idiot as she reached into the cell through that pie-hole and started trying to get my dick out of my jumpsuit all fast.

I was well aware that the nurses made good money doing things like this, but I had no idea Lonnie got in on it with this woman. Her rubber gloved hand fished around and grabbed my cock.

I was hard in a matter of seconds of course, but this was so awkward and embarrassing of a moment. I lost it a bit as she ripped pubic hairs out. The gloves were not letting here able to feel the hairs through the material. It all started to hurt then.

I was not at all enjoying any of it suddenly, but who the fuck says "no" to this kind of thing after years and years of being locked up?. It lasted like maybe 3 minutes. I swear that I had a death-grip on the inside of the door while I had that blue rubber glove give me the most fucked up hand job ever.

Things actually got to the point of me laughing at how stupid and dirty this all was at one point, as I clung to the door desperately hoping to not fall over.

I admit that for all of this torment, how I was aware of going without a woman for 18 years or so up to and counting that very moment. I was not able to let a little thing like my pubic hairs being pulled out in her fist to ruin it all!

No, it went really badly as far as a sexual act goes, and I felt really fucked in the head afterwards for days.

I honestly do not think that if Busthead had bent me over inside of the day-room and force-ably eaten my asshole, that I could have felt any more away from it being sexy

I even closed my own pie hole up and walked away from the door after she wiped her blue glove on a hand-towel before then dropping it beside the bucket that Lonnie was standing next to.

Lonnie came over to my door and spoke to me through the side of the door-crack then.

He said: 'Yo Nigga, how you like *THAT* shit'?!

I said: 'Man, that bitch ripped my shit up'!

He laughed his ass off to that said back to him and as he was leaving he said: 'I guess you got all that white girl "pussy hair" on your dick, and *that's* what your problem is'!

I told him to suck my white girl pussy then, and to then get off of the fuckin' floor. I tried to hold my shit together from laughing but it was useless.

My groin was burning from being roughly abused and despite how funny it all was, I managed to get past this without letting it ruin my break from Death Row.

Lonnie told me Sunday Morning how he would be back that night with my "pkg" to take back to the unit. He said I better not fuck this up, or we were *both* done in this place. I just lay on my bunk wondering how in the fuck did I always end up in the craziest of shit. I was laughing at how I ended up being the prized idiot in a game that was being played on me by guys that I did not really know.

And here I was thinking how I was the one being clever by pulling strings on others in this place with Bobby and Rump...

That Sunday night I got a 12 inch long by 8 inch wide by 1 inch thick molded plastic parcel tossed through my pie-hole. I was not at all happy with it's size and from the feel of it, I knew it was bad news if I got popped with it. I told Lonnie that he was a dick and that if I ever got off of Death Row someday, how I was gonna bust him in the head if I got caught with it. I told him this the same way I was wishing him well on his journey.

He told me to stop being a little bitch in response, and said that if I did not get what was meant for me out of the pkg from the guys on my unit receiving it, that we would crack heads over it together.

In other words, he was saying that I was on my own and fuck it, at least he got me a hand job from the nurse.

Gotta love a guy who is so shrewd that he had you all along. Lonnie just tried to make you like him as your buddy even after he played you for a sucker.

One last item Lonnie gave me Sunday night was the plastic bag with 4 liquid laxative shots that were inside of it. They were in 2 ounce individual cups that are sealed shut like coffee creamers.

Drink one of these laxative shots, you are good to go. Drink 2, it's an all day sit-down on a shitty throne. Don't go past 2. I handed him back 2 of the cup packets and told him how he should have a toast with me. Lonnie grabbed his dick through his trousers and told me to go fuck myself white boy. He handed me back one more of the cups and said that it was in case my dumb ass spilled one. I took all 3 later just to make sure.

I miss that crazy bastard. He stuck by the code of being a 'prisoner' is all that I can say about him.

Lonnie was not an "inmate" who tried to be comfortable. He did not play at being a "con" either. That is where you took on some bullshit "Bushido" warrior attitude to hurt others. No, he was a "prisoner". That is the guy who knows that he don't belong there, but is willing to grow or master it all none the less.

For Lonnie, he ignored what the "man" said you did to be next to him in a cell. You were dealt with as fairly as anyone else. In this way, you got treated as fairly as a con artist such as Lonnie figured that you deserved based on his evaluations.

I had to respect him for how Lonnie did his time...

I had to get back on the game though, so I was sure to drink the laxative juice at about midnight. That way, I was ready for my nasty performance by 8:am. I knew this was going to be filthy work once again and I hate to think of how I had to walk a long way while covered in my own shit to pull off this stupid move. Oh you know I was getting nothing out of it all too, so this is what made what I did that day all the more of a total waste of time.

I could have done all that coy shit where I left that to the end, about me getting nothing from the package, but that ain't really important when I think of how all this stupid effort left Lonnie dead.

It also made me really ready to deal with Roland over it.

So I get the drinks down and I wait for morning. Frick and Frack show up about 10:am and I am in so much real pain in my guts from trying to **not** shit myself, that I actually did struggle to hand them all of my clothes for searching.

I had the package by the toilet and after I did my "I got nothing on me" strip dance (that alone actually had me nearly shit myself again doing so), I had secretly slid my foot over and snagged my parcel with it. I slid it with my foot to the door right below me.

I scooped the package up off the floor by dropping my jumpsuit as it was handed back to me and letting it cover it from sight as I let out a nasty stream of farts.

I actually stuck the jumpsuit with the now hidden package within its folds back onto the pie-hole for them a second time and said to the guards: "WAIT! I GOTTA SHIT!" I then let all of this diarrhea out of my ass in as loud a manner that I could into my toilet, complete with groans and everything.

They both recoiled and stood well back from my door while holding their noses while keeping me in sight. I finished and stood up painfully. I took the jumpsuit back off of the pie-hole while telling them I had been doing that every five minutes or so.

I blanched like I was about to vomit next as I said that we had to hurry. I put my jumpsuit on and fitted the package to my belly while they were at least 5 good feet back from the stink that I was causing. I made sure it was all smoothed down in front with my hands before I stuck my hands out for cuffs.

All I had to do now was walk 50 yards to the hospital exit, then 200 yards across the grounds of the prison to the Elevator, and then another 50 yards after that to end up back to my cell. Then it was over.

First, as soon as they got me belted cuffed and out of the door of the hospital cell of which I was in, I shit my self one last time hard before they touched me in the doorway.

I really did not have to try hard to make this God awful liquid and semi hard substance to gush out of me in a flow. I felt the entire back of this white prison hospital jumpsuit turning brownish wet from the waste that was now running down my legs.

Frick and Frack were pulling me as fast as they could, all while yelling for everyone to get the fuck out of their way in the hall-ways of the hospital. They then yanked me so hard across the prison complex that I nearly got hit by the food cart which was coming out of the unit.

When the food cart nearly hit me that nearly caused the package to come out then from my waistband where it was tucked. I was panic driven to make it then.

It was about 10 minutes of nerve wracking time, where I had to keep right on shitting myself all along with this walk to keep it real.

I lost all control of my bowels from the medication which I had taken way too much of. Along with this the fear of being caught was not helping either.

Shit was literally soaked through the whole back of my jumpsuit as I crab-scampered along with my two fired up escorts propelling me.

My paper hospital shoes were falling apart from being soaked in shit and I had one of them drooping off my foot. I tried to drag it along in a miserable effort to have some semblance of dignity left of at least wearing shoes while covered in shit.

The whole elevator floor was soaked with my feces. My companions on the ride with me said that they were making me clean their boots with my tongue later. They were as angry as I had ever seen them in this place. I was so close to laughing and or pissing myself in fear that honestly, I don't know how I ever got out of that elevator.

By the time the doors opened on that top floor I just wanted this nightmare over. I forgot about all that "hunched over because I am so sick" walking.

I made a mad dash for the cell meant for me with my boys Frick and Frack yelling that the control officer better have my fucking door opened, "NOW"!

They took my cuffs off while trying to extend their arms as far away from me as possible.

As I started to take my jumpsuit off to start handing them my clothes for them to then search each item, they shouted for me to stop. Then my boy Frick walked over and he kicked the pie-hole shut on my door with his boot. They then both told me in unison to sit there in my cell and suffer like a dog with all that stinking shit all over me.

They then walked off the pod and I started to peel my jumpsuit down and off of me with my heart pounding. The package was right there on the floor as it had actually finally slid out and had landed right there by my feet in the doorway. Had either guy just looked down at the door bottom then, they would have seen that I had only half hidden it under my foot. That of course being the one foot that had the shitty paper shoe drooping off of it. It now stuck out like a squashed banana that was once in the center an ice cream Sundae that had been run over on a muddy road by a car.

As soon as I looked at my foot and thought that way, of it somehow being a squashed Sundae, I let go with a laugh like never before. I just let out all of that fear and disgust at what I had just did to myself all in one burst is what it felt like to me.

Once I got cleaned up I put all of my filthy clothes into a plastic bin bag the guards had brought me after Frick and Frack left.

I got the package all cleaned up in my sink with soap and water before I then put it inside of two potato chip bags and sealed it with tape. I then slipped all of it into a bigger bag that came off the loafs of bread that came in the unit on the food cart. I wrapped it all up in my filthy clothes, made it into a big nasty ball and then I pushed the intercom button for them to let me fling it out of my cell.

When I told the guard in the control booth that I had my hospital clothes to be put outside of my cell as they had ordered me to do, he told me to put them in the trash can that was located by the door of the pod exterior and not to come fully out of the pod. He then remotely opened my door and one of the pod doors at the same time which had the trash can next to it. I put the package and clothes in the trash-can under the watchful eyes of Roland in the first cell. I saw it then. He just knew I was up to something.

That trash-can was going to be fished through by the worker on the unit who was there after the last meals to clean floors. He got it out at some point and he then slid it to the guys on the pod with the JBM boys living there.

I got word from the worker by him tapping on the pod windows later that it got there safely.

I had a shower and was in my cell by the time I got word, so I just lay there wondering if this was now the start of something else with Roland going to the guards on me or if I was just done with things.

It took 1 day for me to wait and see how Roland had indeed put 2 and 2 together. My cell got searched right along with the whole pod of cells on the other side of the unit where the package went to.

Curious how that was supposed to be not noticed, but only *my* cell on our pod was the only one searched that day besides a whole pod of cells. The whole other pod where the package went to got stripped bare as well. I sat in my empty cell afterwards fuming because Sgt. Rage took all my belongings and I knew then that Roland had gotten all of us busted.

I was served with paperwork that said I had a balloon with a note secreted within it that was found in another mans' cell, all claiming that my portion of the contraband as being whatever was in that item by half.

4 guys besides me that came from the other pod then had all of their possessions taken off of them for 90 days of disciplinary time. I watched Roland smirk at me as he passed by my cell for days in triumphant glee.

What happened to Lonnie? He got taken to the disciplinary cells under the Death Row unit that I was housed on. He had his teeth broken during his questioning by the guards then, but never told who it was on the staff that had brought the drugs into the prison for him to then send in to our unit. He got a year of disciplinary time in the hole for that.

Well, Lonnie finally got electrocuted in the "electric chair" (as he was once sentenced to die by back in 1984 by the courts) in Pennsylvania. It's the craziest way anyone can die, but the facts are there.

Lionel Baker, A.K.A. "Lonnie" was electrocuted sitting on his toilet while inside of his cell in Pittsburgh Penitentiary.

An inmate who had broken open the wiring of a TV set inside of this same cell Lonnie shared with him then put the bare wires across the metal toilet seat somehow. This crazy wired up toilet was now a live charge.

When Lonnie sat down on the toilet in his cell and urinated while sitting there, he closed the circuit on this death trap. His urine became the conductor of 220 volts of electricity through his body that then killed him instantly. His dick was fried off they said. I could not imagine a more horrible way to die in your cell even if that last bit about his dick is bullshit.

No one was charged in the death of Lonnie. The news story says that it was a hair brained inmate doing a botched job on the TV set, and how it was all due to being wired to the toilet, but that does not make sense if you ask me.

I do not know what happened in his cell, I just know it was a horrible way to die after you had made all of that effort to not be fried in the electric chair by the hands of the state.

What really got under my skin was how I heard about Lonnie dying. Fucking Roland came back from the Lieutenant's office one day all loudly calling out to me. He was crowing about my buddy Lonnie got "Cooked" in his cell right downstairs under us. Roland shout that he was 'Just wheeled out dead on a gurney from out of the disciplinary cells below cooked to a crisp'!... and yada, yada, yada...whatever asshole.

I waited for the investigating officers to come pull me out of my cell and speak to me about his death. I hate "I.I.D" or the "Internal Investigations Division". They are the big brother of the kid who just split your lip open in the school yard. You are suspect for anything done to *you,* is how it goes with these people. They never bothered me this time though, and I was happy for that fact. I don't even think that they spent 10 minutes investigating Lonnie's death actually.

It was such a funny story to them all that they did not care about Lonnie like he was not worth more than a joke to consider.

One thing was becoming more and more clear to me as the days went on in my cell with nothing in it. All while I sat listening to all the guys around me having a blast with music and books or TV. It was this one thought:

Either Roland or I had to go.

Now, I had no other prison within Pennsylvania that was willing to accept me right then, so I figured that I was going to have to make a move on him.

What I was not savvy to right then was how he was already like 2 chess moves ahead of me in our game. He was thinking the same thing that I had just came to now think of this situation, but he had help.

So Lonnie goes to his grave, I do the walk of shame with shit all over me. All I get out of it was some new paperwork plus all my shit taken from my cell for like 90 days. Rump looked so much smarter than me right then folks, he certainly did...

6 'THE RAZOR TANGO DANCE'

I finished serving my disciplinary time in style for Roland's snitch-work. I bartered for the use of a small AM-radio set and the use of one half of a set of headphones that I got off of Yahti. He charged me a fortune and he even made me buy new batteries later as well for using his radio. I liked him for being such a little tight ass who was always trying to hustle everyone. I did not complain about it to him. I was able to listen to the BBC world service, or I could hear college football games or even some music on my radio. So I did an "easy time" once I had some new books sent over to me from guys whom I had bartered with on the pod next to ours.

Even George sent me over some of his food in exchange for my citrus fruits as well as my breakfast honey packets, as he was making "Mead" from the honey,or other wine from fruits. You can do your time hard, or make life passable is how it goes for some.

Once I was back on routine with the other men I skipped yard and day-room altogether for weeks. I was dealing with all sorts of drama in my case and my personal life outside was a mess.

My lawyers that were appointed to my case from the Federal courts were about to do me dirty. I had finally gotten to the Federal court level of my appeals process. It had only taken me 10 years of appeals to get to this level of appellate courts in America. That was after 8 years in the "State" appeals court that were a complete waste of time. My escape from custody made sure of my State court appeals not having any chance. Here was the issue:

I had to have my head shrunk finally by teams of psychiatrists, after all of these years of incarceration. Done by a team of doctors hired by my own lawyers no less.

Not only did I have to have my head "done in" by a team of shrinks that were bent on digging deep into this head of mine, no sir, I *also* had to have this news all delivered to me in the shittiest way possible.

The deal was that since I was raped at the age of 7 years old and how my attacker had beat my head in with a rock, that this could be used for me to get off of Death Row I was told.

All previous lawyers assigned to my case knew going in that I never once made any effort to ask for any lesser of a sentence than what they gave me at first. **Death.**

I knew that this all was going to be a pathetic thing to do to me, where essentially my lawyers say to the courts; "My client is innocent, my client is innocent, **but** if that is not enough of an argument, then let us tell you just how he is broken minded from all what was done to him as a child.

Just so that the courts can accept that I am actually guilty by this type of pleading and accept that because I am so pathetically broken mentally, that they spare my life?!

Fuck that. No way was I ever filing anything like that with a court, where I begged any one for my life only because I then concede that I have no mind left.

Now I ain't giving up no names on who it was that this happened with from my lawyers side. Simply because I love these people who represented me on appeal. I know I could indulge here in this book to point out who did all of this to me, but despite *what* they did that gutted me personally, I am still grateful for my freedom today.

Like I pointed out though, I had to deal with a lot of issues in my time while being incarcerated like this sadly, and each time I try to take the high road over those who tried to belittle me.

The one issue that I had to work my ass off to be at peace with most were the times that lawyers either treated me like I was actually guilty and sold me out, or they treated me like I was insane.

The second group of lawyers whom I describe of this group were the ones at who times that told "Innocence Projects" to use their resources elsewhere, as I was not right in the head, that my efforts to use DNA were a ploy of mine.

A reporter from the Delaware County Daily Times Newspaper told me that when he tried to ask Innocent Projects about my case, that he was told many times how my lawyers told such groups to pass me by because I was insane. I knew all of this even before I sat down with the Federally appointed lawyers who were now "taking my case in a new direction" with these doctors.

My visit with my lawyers about this issue went badly right from the start. The messenger of this news was a guy whom I really had no time for. I get it, you are bright and you are a good lawyer, and whatever else is true about you sir? You were wrong. You were wrong to make me have to go through a battery of Psych testing just for the purposes of using it against my wishes in court.

What hurts is how you made me do this only for the money needed to pay for DNA testing. I knew all along how you were thinking secretly that if the tests are inconclusive, that you were going to ask the court to spare my life due to my brain injury as a boy making me insane or diminished.

I was being fed a shit sandwich right then by my lawyers and told to swallow it down and I knew it. It was all about how they had a this "ultimatum"" for me, too. That was: That if I did NOT go through the many hours of psych testing which they wanted me to endure, how their office was simply not paying for any DNA testing while my case was in the Federal courts.

As I sat in the visiting room with some guard behind me listening to all of my dilemma over the phone system, I was betting that he was probably laughing his ass off at me right then. I fumed silently not wanting to add to his glee.

They had me. The lawyers knew knew it. I knew it, and the guy on the phone in the visitation chair next to me with his hip-hop dressed up white girlfriend (who just popped gum into the phone lines for the 50th time), they knew it. I was sat down like a stooge and I was fed this crap by my lawyers this way, when all they had to do was call me and do it from their offices over the phone lines.

I sat there with a stone cold heart as I started thinking maybe I'd do real dramatic shit on them right then... thinking maybe I should I just say "fuck you".

I knew though that if I said this to them that I was to dash any remaining hopes that my mother and father had of me getting out so I bitched up and tried another way.

In the end, I put up enough resistance to save face. I let them get to a point in this shitty conversation where I let them have their way, all so I could get it over with. Because truth is, they never respected me for who I was as a man anyhow. I made one statement to my lawyer who was the main one in charge of deciding this all crap for me.

I said the same thing to him that Yahti said to Busthead the first time that Busthead looked at Yahti and told him that his butt looked "Yummy" and he wanted to eat it.

My Boy Yahti had the whole day-room falling apart with laughter when he yelled out; 'Yeah, well you better make me *LIKE* it, motherfucker'!

So that day with my lawyers basically grinding me up, I gritted my teeth hard listened to this crap from them until I had enough.

With my thoughts of silly ass Yahti telling Busthead his line back on the unit to keep myself from having an outburst over it, I simmered down. It all appealed to me so much that I thought I would give it a go on my lawyer.

I then leaned towards the glass of the visiting room partition while holding the phone up close to my mouth. I said in a normal voice: 'You better make me like this'.

I then hung up the phone and went back to my unit, back there to go handle all the other things on that floor which I now had to keep a hold onto. All now while these doctors went to work on my head with their testing in the days to follow.

And yet, that one point *right there* is what got my head messed up about the unit. I never got a break from either my court battles, or of my jailhouse battles at the same time. It never ended. I was constantly under all of this duress from some sicko in the pod, or my own battles to live with the courts hanging over me. If it was not the guards or inmates to deal with, it was things going badly at home with my alcoholic brothers (or family) having all sorts of issues outside. My head was swiveling just to try and keep it all under wraps because of it.

With all of this slow dragging of time by the lawyers in court, or with the courts not caring, or how I poisoned my appeals with escape, I was wearing down mentally there. This new aspect with doctors was daunting.

I was so tired of it all right then, and I went into such a funk mentally, that I began sleeping all day. I was being driven mad by all of this pressure while I saw no end in sight anytime soon. I just "clicked off the lights" inside of my head, and I left for a few months of time while they shrunk my head...

I felt something was wrong physically after a while of living like that. My body was reacting to all of this sleep and lack of movement. I knew it was not the occasional "Seasonal Depression" which you can get from putting cardboard over your windows and having no sunlight directly on you for years while living in the cell. No, I was ill and I got all paranoid because of how Yahti suddenly died right then.

How does a guy whom I am standing there one day talking to in the day-room at his age of like 21, just then suddenly *die* overnight?

Well no one got to him physically, as his cell was locked. No one heard him hanging himself and he had no cuts or marks on him that we could see. This kid never had a chance against something though.

Yahti was not even 22 years old when he died, and yet he had such a gregarious way about him that he was just plain funny to be living next to.

I could not believe he was dead, just like that, wheeled right past me with the sheet up over his face on a hospital gurney...

It was Bobby who made this *his* show then. He wanted his racist ass to make this event be funny to him afterwards. He got on his door later that evening and called George to his door along with him. He did a lame warm up of checking on his little wine maker friend and asked how he was doing. Without care for the reply he then asked George if he had heard what killed Yahti. I knew some shit was about to be thrown out there for us all to listen in on, so I got up on my door.

Bobby smiled upon seeing me there at my door. He was sure to lay it on thick then I thought.

He asked George if he thought anything about the food Yahti was being sent by any of the other guys from the pod...

I said: 'That's fucked up Bobby, don't *do* this'... I knew what he was gonna do. Bobby loved to mind-fuck people.

He was going to wind George up mentally about accepting any more food by doing this but that was not the issue. He was also going to try to convince any of us listening then that he had slipped Yahti some sort of poison in his food that he gave to Yahti somehow.

I groaned loudly at what he was doing then..."Oh come one dude"! I thought to myself; "Is it really THAT crap that you really need to do to us all right now"? I felt like saying it out the door then, but I knew it was pointless.

So Bobby takes George down the "Boogey man lane" with his tale of feeding poison to Yahti and he gets George to sing along with how George even agreed now, yep... that he did indeed remember how he saw Bobby give food to Yahti just before he died.

It was pathetic to hear him manipulate George into now believing that he any saw this. But George said 'yep, that was right, he can recall all of that, yes *sir*', and he complimented Bobby on his move to kill Yahti. George said that from then on he was gonna be careful to check his fruit that he bartered for from black dudes especially...

Yeah well, that was like getting a 4 year old to remember how he went to the Moon with daddy was how it was being done before us all right then.

I went over and put my headphones on over top of my ears as this was such a lame thing to witness. Let Bobby get them to wonder if he killed Yahti, I could care less.

I listened to my music to blot things out and yet all the while I knew what he had done. If Yahti died of some thing that was natural, then so be it. If Bobby murdered him with poison somehow,(and I know that if he did do this),that he did it with no one else in on it.

Yahti's death kind of messed with with me for a while. I hated that fat fuck Bobby for laughing for weeks afterwards, but I never tormented myself believing his bullshit.

All I know is that one day, I am standing there laughing and joking with this guy Yahti, and the next day he was dead in his cell.

When Yahti died on the unit it seemed like no one wanted to laugh and joke about things much any longer. You couldn't even get Busthead to come over and entertain us with his antics during that time.

All of my sympathy had to be put on hold though.

See, I indeed had endured all of those psych tests which my lawyers made me have to put up with.

I went through all of the worst experiences that anyone who had themselves studied 6 years of psychology at university level would know to feel. I knew what was coming by being subjected to extended evaluations in a report written by professionals soon to follow.

I got eviscerated by having to tell strangers how I was raped as a boy, followed by describing to them having been beaten in the head with a stone during the assault, to how it left me with "Aphasia" to deal with. Oh, but that despite that shit and how they think that I am "Brain damaged", how I can do some remarkable things with my so-called diminished brain.

They said I was damaged. I say so what? I believe that regardless of having once had brain trauma, that I can do remarkable things. One is obvious. I have talent as a writer and my brain is lucid. Proof? I wrote this entire book that you now hold in your hands in only 3 days time.

No point in telling the doctors that my brain was this remarkable back then, as I did not want "Grandiose megalomania" added to the 3 final psychological reports which they created. All of the ones that all postured that I was crazy as fuck, or that I was suffering from all the bad things done to me as child. I read the reports. It still stings.

I know one thing for sure from that experience that left me with a sense of self assured thoughts in life...No matter what they based their report on, I was right and they were wrong all along. All of the rest is just me trying to rub in their faces in it now, so I won't bother.

And of course as per my truly messed up life, right after I got done with all of those nasty tests, I learned that all of the biological evidence from my trial that had any evidence on it of any value was now "gone".

This one made it all bleak for me...

You see, I should be bitter as hell that I got done like that. All just so that my lawyers got some psych reports to then help them to file a claim in court asking for me to be put on a life sentence. I should be bitter that I lost all of the evidence from my case so their DNA testing deal was pointless now. I was for sure now stuck in that hell hole that I was living in. I should be bitter for so many things right then I guess. I was going through some bleak shit in that cell and I had to deal with this thing with the Lonnie being thrown at me inside of the jail. I was so caught up I was blind to anything else. And that nearly got me killed in the days that followed my exams.

I was not on my game mentally from all of this shit is all that I have as an excuse for how close I came to dying.

It was a weekday that this incident happened on, either a Monday or Wednesday. I am not sure any longer which one it was. I really had so much shit going on in my head that I was a zombie to those around me during this time. I was waiting for my turn to come out of my cell for me to go into the shower and was thinking how shit it all was for me. I had my soap dish and wash cloth in one hand as I was wearing my towel over my boxer shorts. I sat on my bunk with my head lost in thought. I had shampoo in a small bottle in my other hand that I kept tapping on my thigh. I hate to wait.

When my door popped open remotely, I went over to the area where the shower was and entered.

There at the shower room door on the metal bars I plucked the yellow plastic razor we were allowed to shave with from the bars. I went in and turned on the taps of the shower and then I took off and I set my eye glasses on the edge of the window in the shower. I did not even take note of which guard was on duty in the control booth the whole time as I might have had my shit together better if I had.

All I know is that all of a sudden while the shower is going hard over my head, I heard a door pop open on the pod. I was slow to get my head turned around to see what that was, when I saw a brown blur of a human being swinging at me in the doorway of the shower.

Not punches that they were throwing either, he had some sort of blade in his hand and he was slashing at me with this thing!

I lunged at my attacker and made contact with his head by hitting my head on his forehead with real good smack. As I did that, he fell backwards and his feet slipped on the wet floor. As I went forward as well with him, I ended up falling to the floor with him and I both then getting all tangled up in this 8 foot wide clear plastic shower curtain with me on top of him. I tried to grab him as he squirmed under me but he had baby oil all over him by design so I could not grip his skin.

Roland got his hand free and slashed my face over my right eye with his weapon, just missing my eyeball.

Miraculously I never lost my sight when I got all that blood in my eyes from that cuts while he was still slashing at me over and over. He cut my wrist deeply when I got his arm locked in mine. He tried to cut me with the blade locked between my hands. It was only because the plastic sheet of the shower curtain between my hand and his arm let me grip the blade long enough to pin my body on him then that he failed. As he wriggled hard to free himself all the while I was head butting him over and over.

We were both hyperventilating while being wrapped up in that plastic sheeting. Each of us both were fighting for breaths desperately inside of a minute. I was getting so panicked that I was losing my mind as this fucker tried his best to get that arm free and slash my throat. I was near to my screeching in panic as his arm was getting out of my control.

Whoever was in the control room needed to push the panic button to send in the troops. All the guys on the pod were yelling so loud at us to kill one another that it was now too big to ignore. Clearly it was not a home crowd for Roland though, as most wanted me to kill him. I heard nearly every one who was yelling from their cells all screaming at me to finish this motherfucker.

No bullshit, at the same time that they began pulling us apart from that shower curtain, I passed out from the exertion.

Next thing that I knew when I awoke was that I had new bandages all over my hands and not a single personal possession was left in my new cell.

I had gotten tossed on a pod without a day-room it its center, right next to Gary no less. Oh, and they took all my stuff with no disciplinary hearing processing me, nor anything was allowed into the records on the pod over this incident.

Meanwhile Roland got nothing done to him at all for the attack. He stayed in his same cell and kept all of his belongings. Of course it was the guard that was a former cop who hated me that was working in the control booth that day. It was he who decided to let Roland out of his cell to get me. That is why it all went hush.

I sat in my cell and thought that this was now full on war. I even made myself try to joke myself into a gallows chuckle by hoping the power went out right then so that Gary could go on stage and entertain me for a while.

I lay there with my new scars while I had lots of time to think about how to get out of here. All while I still could leave mentally undamaged I hoped, or otherwise try get rid of who ever else was going to try me next. My friend Gary next door to me did not get any more chances to torment others with the power out. It was time for you to go sir, your own want brought it all about too.

Gary demanded to be accepted as being "sane" by the courts and he asked to be executed right after I was on his pod. It was a real spectacle in the news because the so called epitome of evil was being embraced by his own prosecutors as being now indeed a sane man!

The prosecutors all said; 'Good for you for admitting you were just a criminal who was sexually depraved Gary'.

The usual battles played out in the Pennsylvania courts and was shown on the media during the months leading up to his actual execution. Ol' Gary was going to be only the second man ever to executed in Pennsylvania's recent history. He knew that he was going to be a star in the press this one last time for it all too.

As he walked by my cell on his last day he was heavily chained and escorted by four more of the biggest men whom I ever saw in guards uniforms.

They were all on camera by an additional officer who was holding a cam-corder on his shoulder, just like they did with Keith's execution. I looked Gary right in his eyes one last time as he passed by me.

I have seen cold minded men with guns in their hands who were on the verge of shooting someone who looked like they did not have an ounce of remorse. They would have looked like shaky children compared to him right then.

I have seen men so bent on hate that they emit it like electricity from their bodies. This guy was somewhere between shitting himself now, for knowing they were putting him in "a pit" as he had done to others finally, and he was also showing everyone who made eye contact with him just how much he was *into* it all!

It was that Rock Star performer look which he had about him, you know the one where someone is so "lit up" in performance-mode that they are all wild eyed and excitable on stage? He was bounce-stepping hard against those leg irons on his ankles from this energy, like he wanted to get the show on the road so he was *moving*!

It freaked me out to be that close to his energy. It was like being swept up in a crowd when the heavyweight champ slashes through them all.

I found myself taking a step backwards inside of my cell even though I was behind a steel door when Gary had reached me. It was as if I was trying to not catch whiff of whatever mad poison that he was drunk on.

Well, a week after that moment when Gary passed my cell, he was in the death chamber over in Rockview prison, right in the middle of the Pennsylvania Mountains like Keith was moved to. The most gruesome moment was playing out all week, and it was the one that would culminate in one of the most pitiful pleas for mercy ever witnessed during an execution. No one could have imagined what was to unfold and to this day, I still have no idea why it was done.

Some nameless lawyer, in some law offices one day, came up with a brilliant idea to try and save Gary from the dead man's call. He *or* she decided to create one *more* victim for this sad saga to now eat alive.

You see, without truly caring that what they were about to do as far as it's collateral damage to others, they had simply picked out a fact about Gary that they felt could sway the Governor of Pennsylvania from killing this man.

They went out and found his beautiful, young bi-racial daughter.

This girl was the very first child who was born from the rape and torture of the very first woman whom Gary had signed out of the mental hospital, way back in 1979 that they got in contact with somehow. They convinced her to come forward and plead for Gary's life as well...

I saw the news broadcast of this little girl being swept up in this shit, someone who was not even yet 20 years old at the time, and I saw how she began pleading in the press for her "daddy" to not be killed. It broke my heart to see someone used like that.

For her to try and say to everyone that no matter how evil he was, nor how mean that he had been to her own mother, that she wanted to love and forgive him?

That was enough sadness right then that I cried so hard that I had to stop looking at TV all day after that. I was so angry at those lawyers for using her like that. Sorry, but there are some things you just don't "go there" with.

When I think of the newspaper photos of this poor girl surrounded by lawyers who personally did not care what they were doing to her, I felt like they were just as cold as Gary in what they wanted. All I could honestly do was think of what this girl was asked to do.

I can not know now what it is like to plead for the man who created you in so much horror. I could never hope to have that type of compassion inside of me I admit. Nor do I think that I can find that sort of willingness to believe in good until that day when she spoke. I was so proud of that little girl who had to show us all in her words, that no matter what, we have no right to kill one another. That regardless of what we hold as a "right" to do so, killing is never righteous.

The Governor of Pennsylvania was a right wing Republican candidate at the time who thought he would be the next President of America. He had already put one of my friends on Death Row down, when Kieth went to his death in 1995, so I knew he was going to have no moral issues putting Gary down.

A lot of this is next part is well know in the press and this easy to look up.

And so it goes that Gary was bent on carrying out his last comments like he did to us for 9 days when he was to be finally executed.

He was going to tell his death audience before him all about his "glorification story", just as he had done to us in our cells when the power was lost. He was going to have all of these others present before him on his last day to all know one last time, all about his blessings from God to do all the things that he did to other humans...

So, they shaved him where they had to put intravenous needles in his flesh, they stuck him in a hospital gown while they put a catheter in is penis as he lie there on a hospital gurney. They put a heart monitor on him as well then, and then then they wheeled Gary into the death Chamber along with 6 officers rolling him into it the execution's last stage.

I know without doubt that his heart was beating like crazy when they finally got him in there and they set the needles in his arms. Especially so when they hooked the drug lines from the needles inserted into his arms up to receive the drugs to kill him.

I know they had a methodical and detailed manner in which they set him up for his farewell like that. I bet you anything that he was sacred like a child right then from it all being done to him.

But moreover, I bet you any money wagered that Gary shit himself when they raised those curtains and his daughter was standing right there for him to look at.

Way it goes from those I heard it from, they all say that Gary completely lost it mentally at the sight of his child. Said he was blubbering about how he wanted his baby girl to forgive him.

How pitiful is it, that how for all his nasty contrived bullshit, that it fled him in his last moments. He broke down for the love of a child which he had made in his sickest acts.

I felt for his child surely as anyone would, but I just could not feel for him. He was so driven by his own madness that I don't give a damn that he all-of-a-sudden thought now, that he felt something of a love for a child which he had produced during rape and torture anyway.

I just wanted his voice out of my head for good. I did not want him to come back and be in the cell next to me any further is what I thought.

Where they took him was no concern to me otherwise. I sat on my bed in my cell on the top floor of Western State Penitentiary's Death Row unit and I said: 'Fuck you Gary, your whole act was bullshit anyway'.

People wonder why I am not screwed up in the head from my living around these kinds of people year after year. There are times when I just don't feel like I have the energy to tell them my reply to this in detail.

On so many levels, it was *so* crazy that I had no choice but to be drawn into it all.

I confess now that back then, (just as I am now), it all fascinates me to know about this whole other world of Death Row. I mean it. The general public on the outside sees the notorious killer being finally captured on TV, or reads of it in the Newspapers.

People even watch their gruesome stories on TV while munching chips and a cold drink while they are able to consider it all in a detached manner from their living room sofas. Me?

I ended up sharing my snacks or meals right along side of these twisted bastards for decades.

That "guy" who scares the shit out of you at night on TV is standing in front of me when I have to leave my cell.

He is the guy that I had to live with while I had to either befriend him, or alternatively I had to make sure that I never turned my back on him. It was all so real for me like that.

As Gary went through his weird death march it all seemed like a segue into what lie ahead next for me, I was losing touch with hope while I was turning bleaker in my thoughts. I even told my spiritual adviser to take all of her bullshit and leave me to it for a while. I had no time for what happened *after* I died, as I had too much shit going on before I got to that point I told her.

7. 'GET THIS SHIT OFF OF ME'!

Ironically I was once again in the shower over on my new pod when this next incident happened.

A replacement unit Sergeant told me to get my white ass out of there right now, as he then ran onto the block and checking each cell for an inmate to be inside. It was nearly 2:pm and the 1:pm general prison population head count had not been signaled as being cleared by the daily prison horn be set off routinely with one blast.

Instead of that usual one lone blast, we all heard that long wailing noise of the escaped prisoner/ riot horn. If you go back to the news accounts of the time, you can read how what seemed like half a prison block had ran away from the prison then!

Eventually after a few hours, the staff of Pittsburgh Penitentiary found out that as many as 9 men had tunneled out of the prison using power tools. They used drills and all manner of stuff which they had acquired with the help of some really lame industry workers.

Who are theses people that are called "Prison Industry Workers"?

Let me tell you how come local communities love prisons in the first instance.

You see, it is not just prison guards who work inside of jail, there are hundreds and thousands of prison "Industry/Maintenance" workers who also enter a prison each day. These folks are as powerful as the guards.

Back in Huntingdon I learned that the guys who worked as supervisors in the Kitchen warehouse had coincidentally also owned a restaurant in town. It was so easy to load up off of the state with free food when the captain of security has his brother take truck loads of food out of jail marked as "garbage" that instead went right into his kitchen at the restaurant.

The guy who ran the wood shop also had a side business for furniture repairs. The guy who ran the farm on the prison grounds had a cheese business that sold all sorts of dairy products. The guy who ran the commissary for the inmates inside jail double billed everything sent in so that his local store had free stock.

The whole thing is a racket.

The only thing that ended up ruining the millions of those dollars which were getting stolen at Huntingdon for years was the accidental making by security officers of a sex tape. It was all undercover recorded by the security personnel who were watching the warehouse Supervisor having sex with inmates who were working there. The inmates themselves were stealing items from the warehouse in exchange for sexual favors.

It was so rampant at Huntingdon prison where I had just come from that the Deputy Warden of operations was even bounced off the job for embezzling something like $200.000.00 thousand dollars of funds from the prison.

America does not realize that there are a hundred ways to rip the state off through a prison, and how is done all the time is so easy it's a joke really.

My point to all of this, is how I found it incredible that not one person from the "Prison Industry" got fired for having 9 men escape. Oh a couple of administrators of the guards got shuffled around to other prisons, but the industry workers all kept their jobs. That's power.

I got to see the Governor of Pennsylvania land his helicopter right by my window on the big parking area below me after the escape.

He came in there to have his look at the 40 foot tunnel which no one noticed being dug for months and months with the press in tow to show how angry he was.

But heads hardly rolled over this big event, and things were just on lock down for a long while, as every single cell inside of Pittsburgh Penitentiary now was to be searched. It was going to be two solid weeks of no yard, no day-room, or no phone calls home. I went to sleep and waited for at least half my belongings to be tossed away (as always happened during searches) every time someone escaped, or we had a riot to clean up after.

When things happen somewhere in the jail that is this big they trim the fat from the whole of the prison with a massive search. Once they take everything they can from you, they then chuck it all into giant carts to be tossed away...

It was actually these men who had escaped from the general population that became the link to my getting out of this place in yet another weird way that cannot be made up.

It had to of course be all down to the one guard who was tormenting me this whole time. He was finally getting bored of his usual effort to make each day really dark for me. How did he do it? Why did he do it? Roland finally got me set up right.

It started with my food. You get fed twice on the day shift, and then you get fed once more on the evening shift. Breakfast usually is at 7:am, and then you have lunch at about 11:30 am. If the guard who is feeding you on evening shift hates you, he spits in you meal or clears his nostrils into your food once that day. Having it be a guard on day shift do this to you though, and you have lost both early meals each day.

You did not have to do much to earn the title "My Favorite Rapist-Murderer" from my tormentor. I counted the men there with similar convictions like my own. At the time in which he was spending feverish amounts of time tormenting me alone, I was living on a unit that had at least a dozen or more rapist-murders (and even some of them were multiple repeaters of this act) so I was not rare by any means. I was not singled out for my crime. I was singled out because of the dirtiest of lies.

Roland was so good at his con game on the guards that he managed to get lots of time hanging out with them in the Sergeant's office. He would be in there chatting with them about whatever he knew to tell of prison shenanigans which he claimed were going on . It was that opportunity of his snitch work that let him snag a photo out of a work folder belonging to my tormentor of a guard.

This was a photo of this guard's grandchild taken at a playground. I bet that at first Roland did this thievery for his own self abuse sexually, because that was his thing to do.

But then Roland got his boyfriend Marty to come into the play he was making somehow, and then together they got poor George to be the "set up" guy for their little ploy.

Roland convinced Marty to get to George in the law library and say to him that if he sent me a note asking for "That young stuff", how this would mean fresh fruit which George wanted me to send over to him from my pod. Sure as shit, George did as he was asked and wrote a note and gave it to Marty. They never passed me anything but now had George to say he wrote one if needed.

Marty then made up a typed written note in the law library meeting he had with George which they had claimed was from me to George in reply. They said that this note came with the photo that sealed up in a bag. I saw that note in the guard's angry hand later on at my cell when he was waiving it around and yelling in my face.

I had Sgt. Rage and this very angry officer at my door that day and it was as ugly as it gets. They got my door opened by control and stood in my door way like they wanted t bash my brains in.

Both men were furious at me while standing in my face and demanding answers to what they said I had done. The stench of booze was seeping out of Sgt. Rage's pores of his skin from last night's drinking making me blanch in disgust from the smell.

As he stood inches from my face then his spittle was flying everywhere as he said I was a sick fuck. He said to me menacingly: 'If you fuckin' *blink*, I will club your head in right now'!. Then he steadied himself and asked me: 'Now,did you lift this officer's photograph of grand-daughter out of his folder'?

The blood drained out of my face when I saw my note to George in his hands with this image...I looked as guilty as fuck despite myself then, and he took my recognizing that note as if I had done it.

He bit his lip in fury and made a low sound as he seethed in angry thoughts. He just slid my door closed while saying; 'Oh you dirty mother fucker, you are gonna *wish* I had just beaten your rotten brains out'...

I never said anything in, what was the fucking point!?

Each morning after this event , this one guard who was my main tormentor, began greeting me loudly with his same routine on the pod. It was always the same:

'Gooooooood morning to my favorite Rapist-Murder'! This was then followed by: 'And how are *you* this fine day, you sicko'? Then it was the nostril splatter of snot being expressed from his nose into my food, or it was his mouth full of spit from that nasty morning breath which he would then splatter into the tray of food.

Then, with a flourish (and no coffee for me thank you), he would slam the pie-hole shut as hard as he could to try make sure to send my food tray flying into my cell. He followed this usually with manic laughter after he had shoved the now destroyed food fully into my cell. I stood each time very still and well away from my door while waiting for this to be done to me. I then said the same thing by rote every single time: 'Thank you officer'.

There was no way that I was going to last here now that this was going on twice *every* single day for nearly 1 full year. No bullshit either. Each day the same thing over and over, followed by the "Thank you officer " words of mine.

I figure at first that is was a maybe few weeks that I would endure this shit, a couple of months surely, but this sick shit went down all day and every day after for all of that last agonizing year of mine there.

What I had to do to finally, to get out of this place without getting killed being or killing someone, was quite sad. I was going to let this creature of a guard hurt me so badly that they would have to get me out of there. I also had to come up with a way to do it with someone big enough getting involved within the prison system backing me, to make sure that they got me out of the unit before it was too late.

Meanwhile, I was so angry at having my food toyed with twice a day that I at times thought about how I could cut this all short. I could just throw my hands up and say 'fuck it all'. I could let all of his torment drive me to just kill this guard right then.

I mean, I could do it to him while never even have to leave my cell because of all of the weapon making knowledge that I have. All I would need is a pair of undershorts and a magazine to kill him if I really wanted him dead...

When you are being openly tortured, it is so hard to not think of some dark things. I had days when I had nothing left to hope for, compounded by a whole gang of folks around me who wanted to see me suffer as much as humanly possible. It all made me bite hard on that poison apple called bitterness. I wanted others to feel the shit that they were doing to me at times. I hate how it shaped my mind during this time to lose caring or feeling for anyone.

My mind came up with so much poison as I thought of the different ways men kill in prison.

I am not the originator of these styles of combat weapons. I learned my shit from others who used them on me mostly. I just thought of ways to refine it as best that I could if needed.

There are 3 basic types of "remote killing tools" which you can make while inside of your cell to lash out with. This is how I learned how to make each one:

First one was nasty to learn.

I was in the Delaware county jail early on into my prison time when I learned how to make a "SNAG".

I was under serious duress from physical attacks in my first few weeks of incarceration.

Being accused of a sex based abduction and murder case at the age of 20 meant that I was to be challenged or tormented by anyone inside who saw me as being weak. It was all due to a local motorcycle gang who's members were locked up with me on my cell block making it worse. They had 5 members on my cell block who were toying with me daily because they thought I was an informant.

With them on my neck each day making my life miserable, the rest of the broken bastards who were also there soon felt free to indulge in all sorts of dirty things on me as well.

On D-Block of the old Delaware County prison where I was housed there were 2 long tiers of cells. 24 cells in length, (and then there was a bricked off area of another 12 cells) with a 2-way swinging door made into the adjoining walls at the rear to gain access back there.

This extra rear area was all created for the section where the child molesters were housed. That was called J-Block. Once you go in there, you are never allowed around other men again.

With 2 cells used as shower rooms, that meant there were 96 men locked up on that block in Delaware County jail.

Within these 96 prison cells were only those men who were charged with murder or other serious crimes. Mixed in with this basic group of men oddly enough, were also those men who had been put there for disciplinary punishment within the prison.

So basically, D-Block in Delaware County prison was as nasty as the state Penitentiary. When you house men in separation status for punishment reasons who have nothing in their cells, mixing them in with the men whom are being put there for their court charges alone, this always leads to bitter resentment. The ones who have it easy always abuse the ones with nothing.

Me? I had nothing and I was one of the downcast. I was treated with resentment or scorn by 99% of the guys there in my first days of being charged.

I was so young that they either wanted to fuck me, or the angry ones wanted to just kill me. Overall they just wanted to make me so miserable that I killed myself really.

In fact I tried to hang myself from such abuse a few weeks into my torture from all the misery that was mine to face alone. Being cut down by a guard and then being told that I was not allowed to "Cheat the State" out of my punishment was so humiliating for me.

It was followed by a week that I spent chained on all four limbs to a hospital bed, left out in a hallway in my own filth because they were making me shit or piss with no bed pan to use.

No, I decided to fight it out after I hung myself that first year. No matter what was done to me, I saw how I had to go on. Especially after my mom was crying in the prison hospital ward at my bed-side while inmates going past to get their medication with an officer "Cat called" at her. Some guys made "cry baby" motions with the backs of their hands curled over each eye in mocking fashion of a child crying at me while my mother turned in embarrassment from their taunts. What a shit moment.

I was not always able to see attacks coming during some of times in jail I was injured. Like when a guy just jumped out of a cell with a weapon and we went at it with hand to hand combat.

I could at least try to put my mattress up inside of my cell when a guy put a blade on the end of a broom handle to try and put my eye out with it. (That hurt like hell when I got jabbed). If I had piss that was also mixed with borax cleanser tossed into my eyes, I might be able to duck or close my eyes as I had to try and do a few times in the past.

What I hated most was the way you could be gotten in very sick ways, ones that you had no defenses from even if you were looking.

By that point, because of the on-going abuse being aimed at me, I was made to come out all by myself to exercise for 2 hours on the block interior. This was done after each guy all had gotten time out for their exercise time in unison during the day. The Captain of the guards said that I was not to be out of my cell when any other guy was out of their cell.

I was set up so cleanly on this "SNAG" effort that it should have actually worked in killing me. It happened as I was called out by another inmate near to the back of the top tier located on D-Block. He said he had a newspaper that he needed me to come to his cell and move to another man's cell while I was out exercising on the block.

Anyway, I went to go fetch the news paper for a guy and I was mid way down the tier (with the guy even waiving the paper in his hand like I should hurry and keep my focus on him)...

I then got distracted when another guy in a cell I had just passed waited a beat and then tried to get me to look at what he said that he had sticking out of *his* cell saying: 'Nick, Look here, I need you to get *this too*'...

As I turned to look over my left shoulder as this new voice calling me, back over my shoulder,I never saw the SNAG being lowered over my head...

I still get chills each time that I think of how I felt the smooth news paper (rolled into a 10 foot long pole) being slid across the back of my neck. I can tell you that the cutting pain of the bed sheet material that has been made into a braided noose on your throat is burning hot when yanked on hard. When your head is then slammed into the cell bars on a guys door while you think that your head is being seemingly yanked off it shocks you to fight then. It shoots terror through you as you grasp at the noose on your neck. I had only one thing that made a difference really.

I wore corrective eyeglasses.

Curry is this guys name. David, Donald, Darrell, I cannot recall any more and do not give a shit what his name was. A fat, nasty, big old black dude from the city of Chester Pennsylvania. He was doing life on a ugly murder of some girl whom he had abducted, raped and then murdered in the 70's. He was like an easy 280 pounds and dark complexioned fat. His hair was medium length "fro" haircut left over from the 1970's. You could tell that this hair had once been pressed and straightened flat.

He had all 4 of his front teeth missing, yet the rest that were in his mouth were huge teeth, so he looked like a giant angry sloth when he talked.

Curry made this thing to hook around my neck by taking news paper and rolling it tight while feeding in more sheets of paper until he managed to make 10 feet of a pole. Now, the pole does not have to be strong, it only has to be sturdy enough to hold out a length of bed sheet that has been corded into a rope. This sheet has been made into a 1 inch wide line with a big noose fashioned onto the end that is about 3 feet in diameter. There is a "T" made of a second bit of newspaper all tied to the end of this pole so that the noose stays open. Imagine the dog catcher's noose on a rickety hand-made level...

All you need to do is find a way to get someone like me to walk down the tier, just passing your cell, and then trick them with someone else getting me to turn my head long enough to stick the pole out of *your cell bars and over my head.* (All of it high enough above my line of sight of course) Once over my head, then simply drop it around my neck and pull.

When this shit was done to me I tried to react fast. The news paper angled poorly so that it was across my head due to my flinching.

Curry yanked on the pole and rope and he snagged me with his noose across my face. The rope which had my head in a ribbon of sheet material that had been soaked in water to make sure it did not break was cutting me deeply.

My eyeglasses got caught between the noose and my flesh on the side of my face, just across the right side by my cheekbone. Lucky me.

The eyeglass frames were driven into my face so hard that the lenses popped out. It was just the plastic frames on there now. I got two fingers in that gap on my face and twisted my neck at the same time. I managed to have the noose under my chin then. I turned forward and around then. I had the noose on the back of my neck and my head was being pulling downwards. The pain was excruciating and Curry had slammed his body down on his floor while trying to bash my head on the bars over and over as I fought him.

I used my knees to brace back from his efforts against the door of his cell and both knee caps felt like they were breaking. He was down on the floor with his feet braced on the inside of his door frame and yanking hard. My fingers were breaking and I have all these twisted up fingers or broken joints in my hands from where he had so much pressure on my hands that it was snapping my fingers one by one.

The guard came down the tier about 30 seconds into this sick shit, just as I was waning in strength. I was doing all that I could to deal with some of the most horrible pain in my hands and face or neck. He told Curry to stop. Yeah right.

All of this was going on why the inmates were yelling at fevered pitch for this guy to finish me off of course.

The guard nervously got out this pen knife from his pocket and started sawing on the rope to free me. When he did that, everyone went berserk in their yelling then, like they were seeing it come to a dud of an ending. They were telling Curry to snap my head off if he could. When the rope cut free finally, my head hit the railing of the tier behind me as I fell backwards. I had everything go white in my eyes and then...

Well, that is how you make the first weapon to try and kill someone while they are outside of your cell and you cannot get your hands on them. I had no hope to do any of that on y pod. I would not waste my time doing this gruesome act anyway, not after having it done to me.

So that brings us to the next one.

JUICE THEM.

You really gotta be lucky and clever to electrocute someone in jail. There are actually 2 ways to use electricity to kill someone in prison.

The first way is obvious as you get a bunch of salt packets from your food, or save up all of your salt available. You then strip off the plastic housing of a TV set (and or just the cord) to begin. You then take the cord and attach the two bared wires to your cell bars.

You then flood the cell floor with water and drop the salt all over the wires just as you plug it into an outlet. Do it at the very moment that a guard touches your door and maybe you can get him.

That one is pretty lame and is hardly ever is lethal. Circuit breakers pop the power off most times. No, the best use of electrical killing weapons is the "BLASTER".

Thankfully I did not learn this one by having it demonstrated on me. I learned this from when I escaped prison actually.

I was lucky enough (or unlucky enough) to land in a very famous prison in the State of Florida called "The East Unit" which located at Starke Penitentiary in Northern Florida. This is where they put me when I handed myself in from my escape in 1985.

I was in that prison for the hottest 6 months that I ever spent in jail, all while locked inside of a cell located over a swamp. I was there only to be sent back to Pennsylvania and I was not to be executed like my neighbor there, the infamous Ted Bundy. Talk about someone who was both a Monster as well as a Madman!

I was in the only prison at that time in the State of Florida that did not allow anyone to possess any type of cigarette matches while within the walls. Cigarette matches of any sort were banned because they were the key ingredient in a BLASTER. Here is how to make this weapon:

Men in that Florida prison took a 2 foot piece of hollow pipe from their beds. They then crimped off one end of it and sealed it over with melted plastic from toothbrushes. They further wrapped it tightly with bed sheet material at that end. That crimped off and now molded end became a handle or base of a shotgun. They got a nail or screw and then made a hole in the side of the pipe above the handle by about an inch. The hole is big enough to fit one side of an electrical cord into it. That is then sealed around with melted plastic so that the metal is not touching wire. The bare wire is packed inside of the charge which is inside of the pipe. The cord wire which is bare has to be set against the outside as well to make contact.

Then come the endless matches and striker bits that fill the pipe. These are crushed up and mixed with the flint stripes that are scraped. This material made of flint that is carefully scraped off of the match books with a piece of metal is very crucial to exploding it. The two ingredients are then mixed with kitchen salt and pebbles along with shards of glass as well. This mixture is then tightly packed into the metal tube until there is enough inside there to set off a good charge.

All you gotta do then is stand at your door or window of your cell, while you then wait for a guard or inmate that you want dead to walk past. In that moment the victim passes the cell, the guy holding this "Electric Shotgun" aims it at your head while simultaneously plugging the electrical cord into the wall socket inside of his cell. Then he blows your brains out all over the cell block tier with the blast. There are "pock marks" all over the cell block walls inside the East Unit from guys being blasted there that I saw personally...BLASTER is a bad one.

That is some next level shit, and I was really glad that I was under so much security in that Florida jail that I was literally placed above the electric chair. Being placed on Q-Wing where they had our cells "within cells" I was safe from all that. Yep. A cell within a set of bars that had a big solid door to shut you in as well.

Bleak. But safe as well from shotguns in the wing of that one jail I learned.

So that brings us to this last way to get someone whom you cannot get to physically while you are locked inside of a maximum security cell. A pair of underwear, a magazine, (and good ol' Tobacco) is all you really need.

Tobacco is so precious in jail. I know it is easy to think of the normal ways to put value on it. The one I am talking about is not them. See, if you mix urine and feces with tobacco in a cardboard milk carton, you can then boil poison inside of this thing.

That carton you fill with these things you then pierce 2 holes at the top of it to thread a string through as a "handle". You hold this so that you can cook it all into a poison over heat. The more tobacco, the stronger the poison.

You take toilet paper and make "Donuts" to set afire while they rest on the lip of your toilet bowl. To do this thing you first roll the paper around your flattened hand until you have about half an inch thick wrap. Pull the paper off your hand and carefully fold the ends inwards so that you made "pants cuffs" folded internally at each end. This is very important as the paper will not give off any smoke at all as long as you fold the paper inwards.

Once you have it lit, hold the milk carton over the flame and boil your poison. A good concoction takes days to ferment. If you can keep adding more tobacco each time you boil this thing about half a dozen times, you should come away with a "tar" based poison.

Then you make your delivery system.

You take the underwear they make you wear on Death Row and start to carefully un-thread the waist band material. You make sure to not damage the elastic part as that is your material that you will braid into a very strong braid. This rubber material when braided is so strong that it will shoot an object up to 20 feet with enough power to go through a simple wooden door.

Take the perfume card from the magazine advertisements and pop both staples out of the magazine spine. You turn these into a cone shaped dart which is reinforced with thread from the underwear around the staples. You make sure it has lots of loose threads to soak up your poison with from the metal tips of the staples being entwined to a point at the tip.

Take more material from the underwear and bind the elastic band which you made that is braided onto the base of the rolled up magazine. You want the dart to be able to go through this tube you created without much friction.

Once you made this tube, practice with slamming the elastic braided cord into the tube until you made it short enough by experience, to have it very strong on impact to the base of the magazine. You hope that this thing can pull back about 5 inches without the dart coming out and being able to aim it level before letting go of the rubber band which is propelling your dart.

When your target comes in sight, you aim for the neck. You try to shoot the dart into the neck while hoping to pierce the main jugular vein. Your hope is simply that enough poison gets into the victim that your doing enough damage to his neck with it combines so that he dies of a combination of both injuries. This is a horrible thing to do to some guard who is handing you a bit of mail at you cell window.

A prison guard has no chance when his neck is only inches from your weapon and you drive that dart nearly out of the back of his throat on impact which sends him choking and gasping on the floor.

That is why it takes a lot of guts to walk past a cell as a prison officer. You can't help but be on your toes all day and each moment knowing this stuff is real.

Now I described the "cheapo version" of this last weapon system using minimal items.

I saw where guys had used a metal spoon to shoot an office in the eyeball. I saw where they got hold of a metal ink pen and shot it through some inmate's neck (and it went right on through) killing him. This weapon system was the one that is most dangerous to deal with, as you really cannot do much about it when it is sprung on you.

It is a God awful sound to hear a man scream as he is shot in the face with a catapulted spear or dart. The only thing worse than that is being jabbed with a 4 foot long florescent glass tube that was broken off and reinforced with wet sheets. I saw one of these jabbed into the eye of an officer on my block back in Huntingdon prison back in 1989. His eye came out and they kept on jamming it into his face over and over any way.

Every day my main tormentor of a guard goaded me by reading my mail to me through the intercom in addition to spitting or "snotting" in my food. He then of course made sure that I got burnt for my exercise or day-room time as much as he could take it away. He did all of this while also telling all of the other officers on the unit that I was "X"-ed. This meaning that he had put cross- hairs on my back, and how they were all to fuck with me as much as possible for him.

When Roland failed to kill me, this guard knew that he was stuck there with me. What he hated mostly was my looking at him and knowing what I knew about him. He could not put on his "I am an okay guy" act with other inmates in front of me then. So for him, I had to be terminated or made so miserable that I killed myself.

I had all of this shit aimed at me day and night while my spiritual adviser pleaded with me to not do anything completely UN-fixable in her letters to me. Talk about asking a lot of me.

I kept going through the self torment of how I felt chump-ed for how I got played into having to have my head shrunk by my lawyers. I went through all the agony while I faced how all of the biological evidence from my case was trashed deliberately. It stole my will to have hope because of how my appeals were being handled by people who did not care about what it did to me mentally.

On and on it was crushing me, and then of course that was when my wife Jacqueline left me in 1998...

I never even brought her into all this shit which I wrote before now because this was about the unit. I felt all along that the one thing which I could do for Jacque was to shield her from all of the things that I had dealt with inside there.

Jacque saw my broken bones, or she saw new scars on my face and body, but I never let on just how bad it was back there. I could not bare to think of the mental anguish that she would have to live with if I described for her how poor George was abused sexually over a phone call during a visit with her. Why do that shit to your loved ones?

So, I protected all of you from reading of this about my wife until now by not using the added sorrow of how I was in love with a woman for 9 years. A woman whom I had actually married during a Death Row ceremony in 1988 believing I would go free from DNA testing.

Her belief in me while I suffered was a lot of what allowed me to keep fighting. I kept all of this sorrow out of this book because no one needs to really know all that transpired in my marriage while I was going through the very worst and bleakest of times in this hell hole. What more could I possibly add to how her leaving me THEN was like the worst timing that one could possibly choose?

I swear that I held back so as to not seem like I was overly stating how miserable that I was made by all of this 3 year ordeal. The only point of my telling you all of this now, is because while this man tormented me on the unit every day, I really had no personal reasons left not to kill him once he taunted me over Jacque leaving.

When my wife walked out of my life, I did this amazing thing. I have told the story many times over in fact...

You see, I tell everyone how I wrote Jacque this really beautiful letter when she left me. I tell of how inside of this letter to my parting wife that I told her how much she meant to me, or how she had taught me how to become a man for loving me. I go into great detail of this moment in films that I have been captured in, or in the memories I share with friends as the stories of my time with Jacque.

What I *never* tell people, and what truly mattered is how I have already told you that these bastards read all of our mail, didn't I? I told you that no communications left the unit or came in without them sniffling through it like a dog seeking treats. So yes, my main tormentor of a guard had some fun with this emotional moment from my life.

This sadistically driven man who was not supposed to be a prison guard anyway, sat in the control booth one day and turned on my intercom for a joke. He thought this a great laugh as he began to read my letter of "goodbye" to Jacqueline. He did so in the most condescending manner which he could contrive on top of it all.

This pathetically broken man who was a guard laid it on thick at times, as he got to parts about our marriage ending in my words. He did so while he chuckled over my wishing her and her "new" man all the happiness that they could find together. My heart was in my throat as I leaned against the wall and pressed the intercom. I pleaded with him to just mail it out. I did not yell or scream, I just begged him to please have mercy, and that I was sorry for whatever he thought that I did to deserve all of this. I begged and I begged long after he had clicked off the switch to the intercom as I was left standing there begging the wall then...

See what I mean? That shit just made me want to get this all over with. I had seen Keith check out of here only 5 months into this stinking pile of twisted humanity. I was already into my 3rd year of this and I was cracking now. I couldn't take it much more and I knew it. I was 450 miles from any family, I had no connection to any reality any longer there with my folks, and my appeals or hopes in court were so bleak that I knew this was coming to an end.

Of course, with my life being what it has always been, you know that in order for me to get such a simple thing as my exit from this place being granted to me, that it just *had* to be complex and twisted!

Thank God that this is now nearing the point where I can move on with my life. That is how I feel after writing this out all for you, my readers who now absorb this. I felt for years like I was never going to be able to tell anyone this one hugely distorted side-track into this ultra insane world that my story took me into. This was the hardest book that I ever undertook to write in life, and yet it is the best thing that I could have ever done at this point in my life combined.

So let's do this. Metaphorically let's get the fuck out of Pittsburgh Penitentiary as I hope to God that I never have to go back to such a dark place again in my life. I promise that even if it is the last chapter that is coming up now, that it is worth it still to know how it all played out to what finally got me out of there. It is after all, what also got me out of jail completely as well.

One last bit of this chapter first:

Every day I had a mantra. A series of words which I said aloud as soon as I could stand upright before my locked cell door. It's not some pretty thing that I stole from someone smarter than me. I simply stood there every day and said to myself:

'I gotta get the *fuck* out of here'!

Well that was exactly the last words which I said to myself on the day that I got my hand shattered in a metal cell door from the officer who was tormenting me on my pod.

That was all it took to get out of this place. 11 broken bones in my left hand that were to be mangled for the rest of my life.

I am grateful that I only had to give away full use of 1 of my hands for the rest of my life is all that I am saying...

8. 'KILL OR KEEP YOUR VOWS'

I miss some things about being in the prison system. I miss how life was so precious at times, that the smallest of things were held aloft as if a gift from the Gods.

I read all of these books once, they were about a man named "33 Rabbit". He was a Toltec King from eons back in time. He was so in love with his favorite drink made of Cocoa, that he declared a law stating that if anyone but his royal family drank this item or ate it, how they were to be beheaded as punishment. Their then heads hung on sticks afterwards made sure that everyone knew why the king said no person could have this treat of his.

I remember how, when I finished that book about 33 Rabbit, how I went over to my paper sacks in my cell which held my commissary items. I got a chocolate bar out and unwrapped it. I stood by the window and ate it while I told Keith through the vents that I was thumbing my nose at "33 Rabbit". He asked me what the hell kind of pills that I was taking today in reply. I told him the story out of the series of books which I had just read about and these Toltec people.

I said to Keith how the same things rang true about power: The ones stopping others with their power are always the ones taking from everyone else.

Keith liked how I described the work written about these people. He read all four books f the series in 2 days after I passed them over to him. He was a demon when you gave him new material to absorb. We shared lots of books that same passionate way so that we could have something to talk about mostly.

I loved talking to Keith. We had some of the most brilliant conversations about the things we read. We talked about how I had this wonderful plan for my death when it was time for me to go that based on the many books which I had read during all of my years locked inside solitary confinement.

I should have kept my stupid clever mouth shut some would say about this next bit. I know now what I did with Keith right before the days when he asked to die. I see now what I did was the "worst thing" that I could have done to others outside of that moment.

This is where I have a hard time with myself still. I beat my stupid ass down many days over this event and I hate how clever I had to be through it all. Yeah well, I am going to tell you one thing which I learned from this experience: "No good deed goes unpunished".

On the night that I spoke to Keith through our vents that then led to him asking to be put to death, I told him what I had in mind for my own death mostly. I told him how I was going to face my death with dignity by how I came to my reasoning for this event. I said that he should end his life there while he still could by doing the same thing. I went into it as best I ever could with my reasoning behind it.

Here is how I saw it all: I was the only one who could kill Nick Yarris. I know that is not a normal thing to say, but it is actually true of both who was Nick Yarris as an entity, and who in actuality could kill him as he existed. My way to do it was to die of course in being executed by the state. But I was going to do so on my terms after I showed them how I had already killed off the person whom they thought me to be.

I told Keith that the many thousands of books that I could claim to have read in my life were now the tools that I was using to have my day of dying. I told Keith how, unlike what he had known of as a life before prison, that I was a fucked up junkie when I got arrested. He was never into drugs or shit like that, so I had to make him see more in what I then explained to him.

So I told him this all came to me when I was 24 years old. I had just been returned from escape into custody in Pennsylvania.

I told him that right then and there how I knew that I had made such a mess of things, that I was essentially dead to my old life after my escape.

And since I knew my life, the one as that of Nick Yarris was over then, that I had only one mission from that point onward.

I was going to work to erase the nasty mouthed, ugly speaking, and ignorant person that I once was. That I was going to replace him with a man whom I loved and respected. I told him that the only way to live through my being executed was for me to erase everything that *they* thought I was before that point in time. It would only be then that I got to prove it all to them in my dying, how I as a broken human was long gone well before they killed me. He asked me how I meant to pull it all off.

I told Keith that I knew when I was being executed, that I was not going to have an ability to hold a piece of paper and read it aloud. I told him that I worked so hard for so many years of practicing how to speak beautifully in my cell for just one reason.

That I did so hoping that when they got me in the death chamber, how I had to have this thing down by memory with the balls to say it all perfectly.

Keith asked me if I could say my prepared speech all at once to him, as if it would be done at the moment that I had to do so. I tried. It was hard, man it was *so* hard to do that in front of him emotionally.

I had my throat constricting with emotion as this guy was listening appreciatively to me. I pictured him trying conjure up in his mind the image of them taking my life before I spoke, all while I know now that he was conjuring up his own death march scenario.

I began my speech for Keith. It goes like this:

'I am nothing to you. I know that just like the neutrino that emanates from the Sun and passes right through this earth, that I am going to pass from your life without much more notice than that of a neutrino'.

'Whatever you think that I am does not matter any more. I have found a way to love myself and respect who I am. I am able to forgive you for taking my life because I wasted it with stupid acts of a child. I gave it away long before you found me and it does not matter anymore how I die. I have been able to finally love myself'.

'I have tried very hard to learn all that I was able to about this life so that before you took mine from me, that I could love everything about it.

'I am sorry that I did not find this all out sooner, and I hope that my family will remember how hard I tried to show them love'.

That was it.

He really thought it was very well done in effort when I told him, even if it was not his way of seeing things he said.

When I told my speech to Keith I flubbed a part doing so, but I nearly did it as good as in my dreams that still come to me now, even though I am free from such days.

Keith said that he was not going to have any big words for them. That was when I knew I had fucked up. I knew right then that I was confirming to him that he was doing the right thing, but then I swear to God I also thought about how he wasn't much more capable of defending himself than George was able to. It really affected him to see what Bobby did to that poor guy in the day-room with his dick. I knew he was too frigging meek to handle that sort of mental brutality of sexual assault. I could have pulled back then, but I was not really able to step away from the feelings of just describing my own demise for the man.

Otherwise I do not think I would have then went and got the Bible out while I shared with Keith my point with him about being executed. I read the following to him only for my own way of getting meaningfulness from it for him:

'Let every person be subject to the governing authorities. For there is no authority except from God, and those that exist have been instituted by God. Therefore whoever resists the authorities resists what God has appointed, and those who resist will incur judgment'.

I then told Keith that he was lawfully judged by man in court and now he was lawfully sentenced by man to die. If he fought his sentence in this light, that he was actually disrespecting God. I said that he and I both were not actually able to pay for anything to society for what we did, we could only pay spiritually for our actions in life by how we died.

He got quiet on me then and I asked only what he thought this was doing to his folks. I asked how long did he want this to go on for them? He never answered me back. He said we needed to wrap this up instead and I knew what he meant by that. I told him that I loved him, but not to be a dickhead and think too much about the things which I had just told him about.

He told me that he was going to sleep and that was the last of it forever with my friend.

I sent him to his death as best that I could I guess. I did so rather than to see him suffer on and on in conditions that he had no chance against. He lived with pain beyond measure daily and he was sorrowful. That man paid enough for all that he did outside. I don't feel the same things that you my reader does about this probably because I lived next to him. I beat myself up only because of things that were not really part of his actual dying really. I have to live with wondering if he could have made it somehow to another prison, or if he could have gotten his sentence cut.

I heard this saying from Italy. It goes:

"There is no justice without life".

My friend was not there with any hope for justice. I made sure that he got what little he could when he listened to me while he ended his appeals. I know exactly how he felt when he went to his death. I know exactly how he felt when he wrote to the courts and asked to be put to death as well. I promise you that I know every single thing he faced when he asked to die like that.

I know all of this because I asked to die exactly as I had taught him how to do it.

I told Keith the truth: He had the power to stop all of this suffering by giving his life back to God. He could end all of this by demanding that his lawful sentence be carried out. I told him that if he was able to love the person that he was right then, how he should care enough about that person to end their misery. That he should do so before it erased who they were as a human being.

I did not get my wish like Keith did. I got "justice" in my life being allowed to go on when I asked to be executed. I got the worst of it so far I say, because life is suffering. We all live under the same death sentence. I had the same "death sentence" hanging over me at birth that I had when the state of Pennsylvania handed me one on paper.

Before we part, one last bit that needs to be explained I feel.

You gotta know what it was that shaped me from the day I entered prison until this point very, so that you know what it was that I was holding so preciously onto. You have to now know why I did not kill that guard.

See, I made a vow to my mother to not only come home to her, but to be something worth bringing home period. I made such a dire promise to her as I lay on a hospital bed following my suicide attempt in 1982. I made a vow to her that I was not going to become a monster like the people torturing us then.

I made my vow to my mother because I was going to show her that whatever it was that *she* went through outside while defending me, how I would make it worth it to her in who I became as a man.

That does not seem like much then, but after 2 decades of hellish living it seemed to really hold power finally. I did not vow revenge for those who did our family wrong. I did not vow to make everyone know my fist on their faces. What I vowed to do was so much harder. Because in order to hold onto anything decent about myself while on Death Row, I had to forget what they did to me first. You now decide if what I was clinging to about this vow (which I alone held dearly onto) in the face of the following litany of events that I had to endure to get to this humbling point...

I entered my first cell on Death Row at the age of 21 only after I was "fed" to the officers who had just taken me roughly off of a big blue bus outside of this building.

I was stood up in a large outdoor area against the red brick wall of the buildings inside of Huntingdon State prison in 1983. I was held there by the guards at the orders of the Lieutenant on duty that day. By being "fed" to them meant that I was allowed to be beaten for 30 seconds with their clubs and boots. It was done by order of this same lieutenant who stood among them.

That first beating was my first payment for whatever I had actually done prior to that moment. That beating was merely to enforce the message just given to me that I was not allowed to speak while inside of my cell. Ever.

After I was stripped naked and tossed into cell number 447 on B-Block. I lay on the floor with my lower left incisor tooth cracked half way down. The inside of my mouth was all ripped up from my teeth being smashed against the inside of my mouth when a boot was grinding my face into the ground. I had an egg sized lump on my head from a metal club blow meant for my back that was now swelling on the base of my head. I had my nose all caked up inside with blood from the kick to the face which I got on my way to the ground. That was before the same guy put his boot on my face to grind it. My ribs were a series of welts, as was my ass cheeks to my ankles. That was where I got hit with the clubs made of oak wood. Both legs were already going black and blue from being clubbed. 30 seconds is a long time for a beat down.

Then my introduction to the mental anguish I was to always know came next.

The nurse came to my cell and had fun humiliating me by instructing me on how to properly fill out a prisoner sick-all slip, "should I ever need medical attention" while there.

I was then laughed at and ignored by the officer standing beside her while I was standing there bleeding before them both. I did not say anything to the nurse because the reason *that* I was beaten to begin with. It was all to reinforce the message to me that I was not allowed to speak.

I would then spend the next 2 years in that cell with out the right to speak to anyone while inside of it. I got frustrated on my 22nd birthday and in a half hearted manner I sang "Happy Birthday" to myself in the corner of my cell. I then got tear gassed by the guards, along with having my ass kicked good and hard. I then had medication force-ably injected into me by a nurse while 4 guards held me down. It was nasty.

If you defied them and made noise, they "extracted you" by force like this, and they put you in deep seclusion while out of your mind on drugs.

This was a process where 4 of the biggest humans beings that can be made to wear padded combat outfits all line up in front of your door at once. A nurse who is wearing a helmet with a face shield is there behind them. She is holding one of the biggest needles you ever saw in your life in her hands, and she is ready to get you with it.

Inside of that needle is a drug called Thorazine or one they use called Haladol, (or some other psychotropic drug) that is going to fry your brain for a week. You know it is coming as they pull the bar that holds your door securely locked. You feel the power of them as this wave of charged up humanity come rushing in and they pin you down. They make sure not to beat you too much as the nurse has to get that needle in you, so they pin you hard while she jabs you deep in the ass with that metal point.

Once the nurse steps clear of it all, *then that is when you get the beating.*

Next came making me a puppet after my next bad beat down. I got beaten so severely for escaping from prison in 1985 that it went on for 4 long minutes. If you don't think that 30 seconds was a long time to compare it to in that frame of mind, imagine who was doing the beating as well.

I got shoved into a place called a "property room" on the second floor of a building just across from the windows of my Death Row unit. Inside of this well lit room were 4 riot gear clad men who were holding 4 foot long metal riot sticks. Giant ants is what they look like. The word "CERT" in yellow is all you see written above their blacked-out face shields. Its the last thing you see when they start beating the living daylights out of you.

The room they got me in had a height that allowed for the men on Death Row in B-Block to look out of their cells and see me there on a brightly lit stage. The room which had 10 foot high windows which were set every 6 feet or so apart, was allowing all those guys in their cells on Death Row to see me "get some" that night.

At the end, I had my right cheek bone shattered in my face, my left retina is damaged for life, my 6 front upper teeth were broken off half way. I as well had 5 bottom teeth were snapped off and bleeding. I had a 7 inch long gash in the inside of my mouth that had to be cauterized with an flaming hot iron to stop the bleeding when 86 stitches failed to stop the bleeding.

I had cracked ribs as well as learning further that I had a lower transverse bone in my lower back broken that night as well. I pissed blood for a week. I have never had a day after that one when I don't endure near crippling pain when my right cheek bone re-breaks in my face. It is deteriorating from this injury, and soon my face will cave in at some point. My left eye gives me instant migraines whenever a prism of sunlight refracts off of metal anytime I go outdoors now. My left eye is unable to handle any direct sunlight without protection of the retina, so I will always have a struggle with head aches.

This was all done before I was eve 26 years old mind you. I then had to endure a routine that was aimed at breaking me mentally on B-Block for 12 years.

Part of this included a monthly effort to make me admit to my guilt and to then give up my appeals to be executed. Each month I then had to tell them where to dispose of my body after my execution. Each month they made me defend myself for not wanting to admit how I had raped and killed Mrs. Craig, all as they sat with horrible looks at me in turn for not doing so.

I was made to defend my being a sane human being while they were making us fight in cages, or they let men get raped in the cages or while in the showers. Each month they sat me down in a room and asked me to give up my lie, face the truth, and then die. All for them who did all of this sick shit to others. Year after year.

As this went on, I had to never stop being able to learn to not trust any other prisoner. My neck has enough slashes to tell me this now. I had to get through so many times where if I trusted a man, that he would just sucker punch me for no reason, and or try to murder me if they could. My worse experience of this sort of attack shows how this factor was as menacing as what the administration was doing to me.

The exercise cages we were made to go into daily are made of metal. Metal bends and rusts. There was a rod that was threaded through the whole line of fences at the bottom. This rod was able to be pulled up enough to be worked back and forth until a length was taken off of it. The guards searched every cell on B-Block twice in a week looking for it when they discovered this piece of fence missing. The piece of metal was 12 inches long, so they wanted that shit back before it was used on one of them mostly.

They did not find this thing because it was actually slid into and hidden inside one of the pipes of the fence located about 15 cages down from where it was taken. It was put there after all these guys passed it over to that spot on the same day in which it got snapped off.

The guy claiming that he wanted it left there outside that day was Benjamin Porta. Ben Porta had been in prison for 36 years at that point. Who the hell was this creature from the 50's?

Ben Porta raped and murdered a woman in Philadelphia. It was the usual psycho sexual murder. The whole story is not worth wasting pages on. Ben was mentally ruined for having done 30 of his 36 years all in solitary confinement. He was a guy that was so violent that he spent 10 years doped up and strapped to a bed.

Really. This guy was laying flat on all fours while inside of Rockview State prison's mental wards for a decade!

Ben had so many years of drugs being used on him that he was out of his mind with delirium by this point. Always shouting and always chaotic, he was off the rails up to 18 hours of the day.

Ben also took "hits" for money. All some idiot had to do was point you out to him while telling Ol' Ben how much coin you were worth and that was it. That was what happened to me in 1990 when this wild maniac went after me with that piece of metal.

Ben got that piece of metal from the fence into the block from the tier worker. He then sat in his cell shaping it. I heard him all night grinding it on the concrete floor doing this. I knew he was making a shank for someone to be stabbed with.

At the time when I heard him doing this noise of making a knife I did not know that Ben was making this thing for him to use on me. I only knew that fact the next time my door opened he tried to use that piece of metal from the yard to stab me in my guts with it.

It happened when we were taken 6 at a time down the flight of metal stairs (that Keith was pushed down) and moved into the shower room.

The shower room was where you had your shot on guys who have no chance to defend themselves. I knew Ben was going after one of 6 guys in our group. Only me and the guy on the other side of Ben's cell heard him sharpening the blade. The other 4 guys only knew that he had a piece of metal somewhere out in the yard. I knew to be alert and I was trying to be on guard during the next shower day.

On B-Block a guard at the end of the cell block tier throws a long bar forward with a thud. 6 cell doors that have first had their individual locks unlatched by staff then all come open at the same time. If you are at the end of the tier right at that moment you are able to see all 6 men who have only towels around their waists come out of their cells. Each with their heads whipping to both sides at once. It is always the same: Look both sides fast, then stick your head out further.

When you do come out, always hug the side of the wall and walk so you can see the guy behind you. Do not stop and keep your hands ready. If you can, put all your stuff in your weakest hand and be ready to punch or gouge eyeballs with your free one.

If you wear glasses, take some string and tie them on good and tight to your head. Do not wear socks as they make your feet slip out of the plastic shower shoes when they are dry.

Make a hole in the corner of your towel and thread a knot into the corners of the towel-ends so that it is secured like a belt to your waist. If you have to, bring a weapon inside of your soap dish or the soap bar.

As I stepped out of my cell though, Ben made no attempt to play any games. He was an old school gangster. He got right into his attack. He shoved the blade into my lower right side and he went to pull it out for a second plunge as I head butted the shit out of his old ass.

He nearly went over the railing on the tier then. With my right hand that was free, I punched him in the throat mostly with about 4 good shots. I then used that same hand to grab his hair on his head and I was yanking his head backward. I was yanking hard trying to pull him off of me as he tried to get the blade out of me. The shank was embedded in my belly so deep it was stuck. Ben let go of the blade as my shots to his throat had him gasping badly for air.

Ben got hit with a club to the side of his head by the guard behind him then, and went straight down. I got popped good in the head and neck by the officer who was beside me but I was only wobbly. The guard then shoved me to the floor face down.

I was screaming that I had a knife in my guts and that they were hurting me more by having me laying on my front. They were pinning me hard with their boots and it was causing all this pain in my stomach. Only once they saw that I wasn't trying to sucker punch them with a ploy, that there was really a shank in my guts from Ben attacking me sticking out, that they finally let go.

When they let go of me finally, I rolled over and lay flat on my back in agony. I then pulled this thin, really dirty looking thing out of me in one hard tug. It hurt like nothing I knew before then. I was up on knees pissing myself literally after I did that stunt. I was curled up due to the pain and I just could not control my bladder any longer. They took me down to the nurses station in cuffs, and what happened next makes me sick to think about it even now. Not for what they did, but the person who initiated it all.

The woman who was this nurse needs no description. If you did time on B-Block between 1982 and 1994 (before this place was closed down) you know who I am talking about. She was in her late 30's then. A mean and spiteful woman who changed to be even worse after the 1989 riot inside Huntingdon.

I was being held down by 4 officers on top of an examination bed which was set up in the "triage cell" that was on B-Block when this next thing happened.

While each guard secured me to the examination table I had this nurse then take over things. I had very little blood coming out from the wound which I was surprised to see. I was in serious pain and my whole right side felt like it was on fire. I was praying Ben did not dip the blade in poison before using it on me.

The nurse went into the room and got my file out in her hands and held it before her. As I lay with my head turned towards her standing in the doorway, I saw her flipping the first two pages back and forth. The first one listed the Rape and Murder charges that I had been sent to Death Row for. The interior page had the warnings for the escape displayed on it, or how I was never to be dealt with "1 on on1 by staff". As she walked out of the doorway and up close to me she nodded to the men holding me down. They then all latched onto a limb and held me a little more firmly to the bed.

Then it began: 'Oh Look, Mr. Yarris has been hurt'! Then followed: 'Tell me, is it bad'?, 'Is your pain really **bad**'?

Soon as she spoke in that supercilious and condescending way that she was addressing me right then, I shut up. No point in being the straight man to a nasty comic is what I have learned.

She continued: 'Oh, what is that object which I see sticking out of your belly Mr. Yarris'? 'Why is that...why yes it *is'!*, "I think that I can see one of the fingernails belonging to Mrs. Craig sticking out of your guts'!!

Then while leaning over she added: 'She fought you *hard,* didn't she, you fucking **pig'**!!

Then, just like this was one of her favorite treats that they someday let her have with fun doing to us "sick ones", this rotten heart-ed woman stuck her finger in my belly.

This woman fished around for an imagined fingernail where I just got stabbed. I screamed until I became hoarse as I begged her to stop. She twisted and then fuckin' turned that index finger of hers, both either way inside of the bleeding wound. She kept right on saying the whole time: 'You fucking sick piece of garbage, I hope they kill your filthy ass'!

I cried like a child and was blubbering from the pain as well as the psychotic things on top of that. I was being slapped in the face by the guards and they spit in my mouth when I screamed. One guy took a whole mouthful of tobacco juice and drooled it into my mouth while he had yanked open my lips with his gloved hand.

I choked their spit and twisted my head awway as they all thought one last shot to my nuts was called for, so then they all did one round of "HOO-HA!" on my balls with their fists and I passed out.

I was put into good old 447 Cell at the end of the block and left there to think about how that creature of a nurse had just gotten off on her own version of "righteous justice".

We are not done yet though. You need to know what it is like to have this same woman greet your mother in the visiting area room and charm her two weeks later.

My mom said how she met the most sweetest nurse ever then. When the nurse asked my mom "how is Nick"? She further asked of my mother did I get the fingernail thing looked after. I nearly told my mom what the fuck they were doing to me when I heard of her being toyed with like this.

I wanted to say things like 'Mommy please save me, please make them stop hurting me'! I wanted to cry and believe somehow that God would let her take away all the shit they were doing to my head. I wanted to breakdown and just ball my eyes out like I was still her little boy, all so that she could protect from bad things...

I cried later though, not then. I kept my shit together. I did the best that I could not to think about how fucked of of a human being you have to be to play with my mother this way. Especially after you did some of the sickest shit ever imaginable to me for no reason at all. I wiped all of that shit from my head then as I told my mom how I was making her a new decorated handkerchief as a gift.

I said that I was learning art designs from long ago and how I was happy to learn this stuff. She smiled then and I got her to never even catch on to what went down with my being stabbed. All while I seeped blood through my wounds under the visiting table, well out of her sight in the visiting booth. I stayed bent over so as to make sure my mom did not see what that lovely Nurse had done to her child I thought...

Look, that has to be *it.* Lets get out of here while I still can pour this out in writing. Even I am sick of it all and want this over now. There is no point telling you more of what I fought through, to then still try and hold onto my dignity. So lets turn off the flames on this burnt offering so that I can move on with my life.

The last incident by my tormenting guard was when he got my door opened by himself, breaking protocol of having anyone backing him up.

He said he was moving me from my cell and putting me next to Busthead. I knew what was up from his smiling face right then. He couldn't get Roland to do it, so he wants me done in by this next guy. I had just about enough, so I said, 'No'.

He said 'Misconduct!' 'You are getting your shit taken for 90 days'. I said; 'Go get the Lieutenant' as I then closed my door by grabbing the pie-hole and sliding my door shut.

As this guard went off the pod and into the hallway, I knew it was coming next. He wasn't going to get anyone else and tell them what I had just done. He went and got a riot stick out of the security locker inside of the control booth. He then came back onto the pod and told me that if I did not pack up my cell belongings that I was going to get that stick shoved up my ass by him.

So I start pacing back and forth in my cell...I was torn between wanting to tell him to kick that mother fucking door open right now, and lets get this shit on...and wanting to figure out what was my best play. I was just walking back and forth, my anger was like steam coming out of my ears. I was pumped up with rage and fear. I was to that point where I was not anywhere near a rational thought. This was all primal and tense. I was going to go off on this guy finally.

This guard now sees how I ain't no more 'passive Nick' and he is not sure that the stick which he is holding is going to be enough. Now he was not so sure that he could handle all the rage that he had been brewing inside of me. He switched tactics then. He told me that he was coming back in five minutes, and how he was putting boxes in front of my cell for my belongings to go into. He said that I better put my shit in them and have my hands out of the door for cuffs to go on when he got to my door upon his returning.

I wasn't putting my hands out defensively. I was damn sure not doing anything he said until I saw someone wearing bars on their shoulders to talk to about this shit. Until then, I was staying in that cell and he had to come in and get me 1 on 1.

My heart was gonna pop from all of this shit as I heard him coming back from the hallway. He tossed the boxes in front of my door, stepped back a step and called out to the control booth for my cell door to be opened remotely. My door popped free of its lock then. I pushed it side-ways, sliding it open fully and I said again: 'I wanna see the Lieutenant'. He said simply: 'Boxes'! I stuck my hand down to get a hold of the first box.

That is when he slid the metal door of my cell shut with all his might, right on top of my left hand that was crushed instantly.

White pain shot up my arm from this and I shook literally like I was being shocked from it all. I have a huge mass of unhealed broken bones on my left hand from this incident now. Every day that I move my hand a tendon "jumps" across it, causing me pain all through my fingers. That prisoner Curry broke most of my fingers with his "SNAG" on that same hand, but the whole back of my hand will always be deformed from being smashed in a door frame. I can use it now okay, but it too has become "My Mistress Of Pain" as I call my many broken bones.

This guard hurting me knew that as soon as he saw my hand swelling up like a basketball that he was screwed then. That was paperwork right there folks. I was going to be investigated because this was a major injury. He raised his club like he was going to go all "In for a Penny, so in for a Pound" on my head with it. I was in so much pain that my eyes had white colors around the edges now. I was sliding down the wall to my knees holding my crushed hand while ignoring him and his words. I don't know why he didn't just bash my head in and get it over with. I honestly do not.

When he left the pod, I stuck my hand in the metal toilet and flushed it over and over, just for the cold water to help numb the pain.

I stayed in my cell overnight and no one came or bothered to follow up on his actions.

I got called out for a visit 2 days later though and the handcuffs would not fit my arm due to swelling. They then called in the doctors and a captain of the guards got involved further. It all blew up inside the unit and I was put on a special bus with heavily armed men within hours. I was driven 60 miles South of Pittsburgh, to where Greene County Super-max prison awaited me.

Sadly for me my main tormenting guard also had a son that was working there at Greene County Prison waiting for me. He had a message for me when I landed inside of that prison later that day. It was simple. I was to keep my mouth shut as I was told to do by his father, or he would finish the job that his daddy had begun.

Now that I am free (while hopefully you, my main antagonizing guard, are a drunken mess in life somewhere), I hope that one day this guard reads this book so that he can see how we all know what a piece of work that he truly is.

I healed from this guy mashing my hand to pulp, but the Hepatitis-C that I contracted back in Huntingdon when they broke my teeth (and turned my mouth into mush) was what I had to face *after* Pittsburgh.

My body began to die. I tried to fight it happening. I got put on cancer fighting drugs that are used to kill this virus which are drugs so strong that I was made toxic by them. It got to the point of temporary blindness with being severely over medicated. The medications damaged my internal organs badly from this. I will have a shortened life span from what was done to me over all, either illness-wise or injury related. So be it.

In 2002, some 7 years after I talked my friend Keith into killing himself, I too wrote to the courts and asked to be executed. I was saved in the last days by DNA testing results on the evidence that was once thought to be all lost. All along, I was not some lying, crazy madman who was pulling a hoax on all the world they learned from this.

My 'punishment' in life for not being a murderous monster or a sick madman, is how everyone always thinks that I am left somehow "diminished" for what I went through. I was treated like I was insane while I was tortured badly while in prison. Those were acts done *to* me, not *by* me to others.

Yet I am now suspect of being possibly insane for having been innocent all along while enduring this torture. It is not fair and it sucks when I have to prove myself to people because of a notion in their heads.

This notion they have of my being somehow off mentally in *some* way is really nothing that I can answer to I have learned. I bet no one else could handle what I have and still be as level headed as I hold myself to be is what I know to be true.

So that brings us back to what I pointed to. I went through all of this mentally cruel stuff with one intent only. I was going to keep my vows to Jayne Yarris as promised her that I would.

I was going to make sure that whatever she got back from their torturing me was worth so much good. How can I ever explain that I set aside my own battle for sanity. all so that I could give every effort that I was as a man to my simple promised words to my mother?

I was going to make sure that whoever put her down on the outside, also saw later how I was a nice man when I got out for this very reason. That way, all could see why my mother had stuck by me all those years. I was going to ignore all that was done to me in a prison cell because of one thing that I know to be true. It is one truth that many will never know actually:

"Freedom" is some made up bullshit.

You are a prisoner to every person whom you ever loved or cared about in life. You are a prisoner to life itself, and a prisoner to all whom you care for, or want inside of your life.

As such, don't be a punk-ass "inmate". Do not get all complacent with the easy way, while you let yourself just be a suck-up to everyone around you.

Don't try to hold onto some notion of being like a "Convict" where you live by some code where you have to go around acting dominant over others.

No, be like Lonnie. Be a good "Prisoner". Don't listen to what the "social world" around you says you must do in order to have an opinion. Pay attention to what determines how you treat people face to face. Deal with them as fairly as you feel they deserve that is based on the respect which they give to you.

The people in your world may not like how you do this at times, but they will have to respect you for being honest to their faces at least. Be consistent. Just be yourself in that way.

I wrote this book for a reason. When I met Laura and we fell in love, I told her then that I had this 'thing' within me that I had to finally let go of.

SHE was the one who asked me why I did not just write it all down in a book. I did. I wrote this work with her watching over me for 3 days while she fed me and cared for me. She stood guard over each tear that I shed until it was all free of me at last.

If you are disappointed that there is no more material for you to read on with, I cannot help that. I am a story teller by craft and this story is clearly over. I think this was one of my best stories to share with you all for what I learned of myself once again. It has to stop now though, because there are no big points left to make. I got out of the unit finally after being maimed, and I killed no one for all of my suffering.

I love it that I finally had enough things in life happen to me as a free man now, that it has allowed me to write this wonderful work at this time of my life. The way I ended up writing it all here in Somerset England, on this pretty April Day in 2016, is so very representational of what I hold myself to be as a man. Be able to accept when you need others in order to grow.

Thank you Laura Ann Yarris. I proudly have your name tattooed on my flesh, while you also carry mine to all in life proudly as your own. Thank you for letting me get this story out in a way that cannot take from me my overall message of development while in prison.

That was such a fear of mine that you helped me with Babe. You made me see how it now does not matter that I share this tale, because you say that so much of it shows how I was a loving man despite my bad days. That you will love me in all of my days that are good or bad because you know I will remain the same inside.

The ending of this work was the beginning of my time with my wife Laura and our children in 2016. I like that. I took the shittiest walk in life back inside of prison, only to now hold on long enough to walk in the elegance of love, all without being owned one bit by anger from it all.

The End.

Post Script...

I am going to say this last thing as best that I can about this book:

Man, I cannot believe I *made* it. I did it. I got through it all and I got to this point where my telling it is somehow the completion of my prison writings. I need not bother with any more prison books now, as all of the ghosts from my past are sheets that are now hanging on laundry lines. Its all sweetly over...

Bye and thank you. I love you for reading this book of mine and no, you are not "sick" or "wrong" for laughing your ass off at a guy with a pen sticking out of his asshole...it's allowed.

With love always,

Nick

ABOUT THE AUTHOR

I was born in Philadelphia in May of 1961. Before me came 3 older sisters and then my older brother Michael as well as my younger brother Martin.
Both brothers are now dead, as is my mother as well. My father still resides in Southwest Philly. I am 57 years old at the time of this work and this is my 4th book to be fully published.
I am harder than life, yet kinder than love. If you understand this notion about yourself, then everything which I have tried to share here is worth it to me for **your** sharing this same feeling in life.

Printed in Great Britain
by Amazon